60 Cela: La familia de Pascual Duarte

Critical Guides to Spanish Texts

EDITED BY J.E. VAREY, A.D. DEYERMOND, C. DAVIES

CELA

La familia de Pascual Duarte

Alan Hoyle
Lecturer in Spanish
University of Manchester

Grant & Cutler Ltd
in association with Tamesis Books Ltd

© Grant & Cutler Ltd 1994

ISBN 0 7293 0356 X

I.S.B.N. 84-599-3366-0

DEPÓSITO LEGAL: V. 266-1994

Printed in Spain by
Artes Gráficas Soler, S.A., Valencia
for
GRANT & CUTLER
55–57 GREAT MARLBOROUGH STREET, LONDON W1V 2AY

Contents

Contents

Preface

La familia de Pascual Duarte is reputed to be the most translated book in Spanish literature since *Don Quijote*. The first English translation of 1947 (*5*) is now a rare collector's item. The second (American) one has been republished (*7*) after Cela received the Nobel Prize for Literature in 1989. In this Guide page references after quotations are to the Spanish paperback now in its twenty-third edition (Barcelona: Destino, 1992). It has the virtue of cheapness, availability and legibility, despite some obvious printing errors (pp.54, 59, 77, 94, 147, 164). References to works in the Bibliographical Note are indicated by an italicized numeral, followed where necessary by page numbers.

My thanks are due to the University of Manchester for numerous Staff Travel Grants, to those colleagues who read and commented on earlier versions of this study — Alan Yates, the late Helen Grant and Leo Hickey — and to Derek Gagen for easing me into the Pascual Duarte slot at Manchester in 1971. I should also like to thank the editors of this series for their helpful criticisms, patience and encouragement, especially when my mind was distracted by other family matters.

The book is dedicated to my parents Alf and Dorothy Hoyle, to my children Emily and Daniel, and to the memory of María (in, among other places, Guadalupe and Torremegía).

1. Introduction: Text, Context and Critical Gaps

La familia de Pascual Duarte (1942) is the fictional autobiography of a condemned man. While in prison awaiting execution, Pascual Duarte writes down an account of his family life as a peasant in rural Estremadura at the turn of the century. His story is punctuated by the series of murders he commits, starting with his dog and horse, then his wife (probably), his wife's lover, and finally his own mother. Although the content of the story is, to put it mildly, rather unusual, it acquires a certain authenticity from its presentation in the form of a manuscript. This is supposedly discovered by an anonymous transcriber, who publishes the text along with introductory and concluding notes of his own, a covering letter from Duarte himself, and letters from the prison chaplain and guard bearing witness to the execution. The text is also preceded by a brief dedication and the clause of a will that explains in part the disappearance and eventual discovery of the manuscript. All of this allows the real author to dispense with a conventional third-person narrator and conceal himself behind the transcriber's notes and the autobiographical manuscript, thus creating uncertainty in the reader about the author's intentions (*15*, pp.282–83). This form of presentation also contributes to the novel's immediate and often enduring impact, for the first-person narrative encloses its readers within the mind and body of a murderer whose life is vastly different, it is to be hoped, from our own, and forces us to experience the vagaries of a personality that lurches pathologically from moments of tender sensitivity to moments of brutal savagery. The effect, at least on this reader, is both memorable and extremely disconcerting.

It is with some relief, therefore, that our attention on second and subsequent readings can be diverted from the disturbing immediacy of Pascual's story to reflections on the more objective context provided by the added documents and on the wider literary

context within which the novel stands. The discovered manuscript is
of course a traditional device in fiction, and it is combined here with
another convention, that of the epistolary novel, since Pascual's
manuscript takes the form of a letter addressed to an unnamed
reader and is accompanied by the three letters and two notes already
mentioned. But as Marañón indicates (*45*, p.15) and Sobejano
demonstrates (*66*, pp.42–45), the most important precedent is that
of the picaresque with its basic ingredients of low-life and a
delinquent first-person narrator. For example, Pascual's description
of his parents and his use of proverbial sayings bring to mind
Lazarillo de Tormes; his opening sentence, 'Yo, señor, no soy
malo', is a variation on the first line of the *Buscón* ('Yo, señor, soy
de Segovia'); and the presentation of the story as a cautionary tale
told by a repentant sinner recalls the moral didacticism of *Guzmán
de Alfarache*. Sobejano also mentions traces of more recent
influences such as Valle-Inclán's *esperpentos*, Lorca's tragedies and
Baroja's prose (*66*, p.47). To these we might add Dostoyevsky with
his interest in crime and punishment, plus a whole corpus of prison
literature which overlaps with the picaresque and includes auto-
biographies by real as well as fictional criminals.[1] All of these
precedents belong to a tradition of serious realism. But there is
another echo, that of the *romance* or ballad tale (*66*, p.46.), which
points to a different tradition of popular sensational realism. Indeed,
there is enough exaggeration, not to say implausibility, about
Pascual Duarte's criminal career of animal slaughter, manslaughter,
assault, uxoricide, matricide and homicide to warrant some
comparison with the world of the *folletín* and penny-dreadful.
Implausible or not, the crude violence of Pascual's actions have led
critics and lovers of labels to regard the novel as the initiator
in Spain of a vogue for violent realism known as *tremendismo*
(see especially *66*, pp.35–40; *71*, pp.95–104; *44*, pp.42–43; *1*,

---

[1]See Zahareas (*58*); and Victor Brombert, *The Romantic Prison: The
French Tradition* (Princeton: Univ. Press, 1978). *Don Quijote* is the most
famous novel presented as a discovered manuscript. A closer precedent is
Benjamin Constant's *Adolphe* (1808) with its 'éditeur' and at the end two
conflicting letters.

pp.xvi–xviii; *9*, pp.34–41; and *39*, pp.15–17). Another favourite link, because of Pascual's moral disorientation, is with French existentialism, and in particular (because it is also the autobiography of a condemned man) with Camus's *L'Etranger* (1942), though the parallel in the latter case is more notable for its differences than its similarities, as Marban's study has amply demonstrated (*46*; see also *44*, pp.47–51; and especially *71*, pp.85–95). Since I agree with Sanz Villanueva that both links are superficial (*63*, p.255), they need not detain us any further. Sanz Villanueva himself favours a tradition of rural dramas, but I think him wrong to see it as more important than the picaresque (*63*, pp.259–60).

Precedents and echoes can be suggested in abundance. Nevertheless, Cela's deceptively simple tale becomes much more complex on a second reading (*44*, p.32) and manages to assert its originality by the way it continues to defy categorization, whilst generating seemingly endless interpretations. The main reason, I think, is because it combines in a very intriguing way three particular qualities: the artistic cunning of its form, the realistic intensity of its content, and a bizarre psychology that crucially and problematically unites the two. This is especially evident in Pascual's relationship with his mother. Matricide, though rare, is not unknown in real life. In literature it is even rarer; the one obvious precedent is Orestes, but this parallel has already been explored as far as it will go (*16*). The matricide on its own is sufficiently abnormal and hideous to set Pascual's character apart from both real life and literature as a special case for treatment and for study. The second quality of realistic intensity arises from the fact that the novel is not simply a lifeless imitation of the picaresque, as was the case with Cela's own *Nuevas andanzas y desventuras de Lazarillo de Tormes* (1944); it is a modern variation which moves from the episodic structure of the originals into a more dramatic form, with a fairly unified setting and an action that unfolds like a three-act tragedy, while exploiting to the full the picaresque story's potential for complex time-shifts between the narrator's past and present. Where the novel shows most clearly its other quality of cunning artistry is in its use of appended documents to construct around the main autobiography an elaborately contrived context. This last feature constitutes the most important variation on the picaresque, though it may well have been inspired by Lazarillo's 'Prólogo' and especially the shadowy 'caso' (*53*, p.90; *19*, pp.94–95), which is 'both the cause and the climax' of Lazarillo's story.[2]

At first glance the added documents are there simply to provide a prologue and an epilogue, making the novel into a unified whole. They complete the autobigraphy by describing the circumstances of composition and transcription, and the death of its author. They also give moral guidance to the reader about the character of the condemned man. In short, they set the main text within an appropriate context in terms of formal structure, narrative viewpoint, historical background and moral response. But when considered on second or subsequent readings, the documents assume a new and more intriguing role, stimulating the reader's active participation in sorting things out (*24*, p.5; *42*, p.37; *22*, p.18), for they contain a number of discrepancies especially in relation to the text they are supposed to clarify. They raise in fact more questions than they answer; and the contexts they supply will pose, as we shall see, four major problems of interpretation.

The most glaring discrepancy, and the fundamental problem, concerns the basic chronological structure. We soon come to realize that the story culminating in the matricide is not the whole story, and that what remains unsaid is much greater than we are initially led to expect. Pascual's covering letter is dated 15 February 1937, but the date of the matricide in the final chapter is 10 February 1922. There is, then, a gap of fifteen years between the end of Pascual's text and the time of writing. And to make matters worse, there seems to be no satisfactory reason for the gap. The trouble with the most obvious explanation (the interruption of the story through Pascual's death) is that it is undermined by Pascual's own decision to stop writing as announced in his letter: 'suspendo definitivamente el seguir escribiendo' (p.16). Even though this in turn is contradicted by the transcriber's assertion that Pascual 'no

---

[2]Alan Deyermond, *'Lazarillo de Tormes': A Critical Guide*, CGST, 15, 2nd edn (London: Grant & Cutler, 1993), p.80.

suspendió *definitivamente*, como decía, su relato', the implication is that the letter was prepared well beforehand, 'con todo cálculo' (p.159). Whilst not ruling out the possibility of the execution cutting short the manuscript, this still leaves the cause of the ending wide open to uncertainty. Another explanation might be that the intervening years Pascual spent in prison after the matricide were uneventful and therefore simply omitted. Though this may have been true of his imprisonment in Chinchilla, it certainly does not apply to the year preceding his death in Badajoz prison. When the transcriber thinks it unlikely that Pascual could have been released from Chinchilla 'antes de empezar la guerra' (pp.158–59), there is (*pace 71*, pp.63–67), a clear connection with the outbreak of the Spanish civil war in 1936.[3] And the same momentous event is recalled again in the next sentence by the reference to 'los quince días de revolución que pasaron sobre su pueblo', that is, the brief period of revolution under the Republic before the area round Torremejía was occupied by Nationalist forces.[4] But the most significant event of all, for Pascual and the novel, is alluded to in the same sentence and in the same casual way when the transcriber

---

[3]Urrutia's contention that Pascual came out of prison before the war is based on a misreading of 'parece descartado que salió de presidio antes de empezar la guerra' (pp.158–59). This is correctly translated by Kerrigan as 'it seems certain that he could not have been released from prison before the beginning of the Civil War' (*6*, p.128). Ambiguity is created by the indicative where a subjunctive (*saliera*) is expected. Three out of eight native informants I consulted first understood the sentence like Urrutia, then on reflection changed their minds. Marban also seems in two minds (*46*, pp.133–34). My reading was supported by the other five and a number of critics (*74*, pp.41, 43; *3*, pp.585–86; *52*, pp.114–15; *44*, p.35; *47*, pp.95–96; *11*, p.592). Urrutia's supposition that Pascual was released in the amnesty of February 1936 echoes Sobejano (*66*, p.22), surprisingly, and Osuna, who still situates the murder at the outbreak of war (*53*, pp.88, 85)

[4]See *12*, pp.371–73. The military uprising which led to civil war began on 18 July 1936. Franco's Army of Africa under Yagüe left Seville on 6 August and reached Mérida by 10 August. There would have been time for a fortnight's revolution in Torremegía, situated on the main road 17 kilometres south of Mérida; in fact relatively little happened (*33*). Torremejía (*pace 71*, p.128) is often spelled thus.

mentions another murder by Pascual, the 'asesinato del señor González de la Riva — del que nuestro personaje fue autor convicto y confeso' (p.159). He then confirms what is already apparent: no details are known about the murder because Pascual has not provided any.

Except, that is, for the dedication: 'A la memoria del insigne patricio don Jesús González de la Riva, Conde de Torremejía, quien al irlo a rematar el autor de este escrito, le llamó Pascualillo y sonreía' (p.19). Given the fact that Pascual is about to finish him off ('rematar'), the Count's gesture of affection is very puzzling and has led some to infer that Pascual must have been administering a *coup de grâce* to the dying man (*74*, p.44; *26*, p.658; *18*, p.122). But this is hard to square with the transcriber's use of the term 'asesinato'(*53*, pp.87, 91). Moreover, one could argue that the smiling face and the diminutive might be interpreted not as gratitude for a mercy killing but as scornful gestures of condescension, in wry recognition that a potential friend is now an enemy.[5] Whatever the precise emotions of the two men are, we have to accept the fact, strange as it may seem, that Pascual dedicates his story to his last victim, the nobleman of his village, for whose murder, we must also presume (*pace 18*, p.125), he is convicted and sentenced to death. Even though the circumstances of the crime are not described, speculation as to their nature is clearly invited by mention of the immediate context of the civil war. Pascual most likely killed the Count out of socio-political motives during the period when revolutionary passions were unleashed in his village by the military rebellion against the Republican government. There were after all numerous examples of this throughout Spain in July and August of 1936 (*74*, p.40). Entrambasaguas is right to suppose that Pascual 'sería puesto en libertad, sin duda, apenas comenzada la guerra de liberación, por los marxistas [...] y él iría [...] a su pueblo [...] para asesinar al Conde de Torremejía' (*3*, p.585).

---

[5] A mercy killing is contradicted by the transcriber and Pascual's plea for forgiveness (*47*, p.93). Even if it were one there would be no reason to omit it. Conceivably Don Jesús mistook Pascual's intentions (*15*, p.288), but he must have known of Pascual's previous record of killing without mercy.

However enigmatic and vague, the murder of Don Jesús is an obvious allusion to the civil war (*44*, p.38; *63*, p.264). Many critics may choose to ignore or remain sceptical of the civil war connection, but it is, I suggest, inescapable.

Even supposing, however, that the killing is explained by the historical context, the main and by far the most interesting problem is to explain precisely why it has been omitted from the narrative (*74*, p.42). The importance of the problem is underlined when the transcriber draws our attention to the textual gap, or lacuna, at the end of Pascual's manuscript, 'la laguna que al final de sus días aparece' (p.159). And it receives further emphasis from the teasing description of the transcriber rummaging around the chemist's shop in Almendralejo in a fruitless search for more pages. If the transcriber expects to read more, then so presumably must we. But our expectations are manifestly frustrated. In place of a conventional omniscient narrator, all we have to rely on is a transcriber who gives tantalisingly brief information and admits his total ignorance about what is evidently a crucial aspect of the whole story. Thus we find that the extra documents supplied by the transcriber neither complete the text nor close the novel; instead, they reveal the incompleteness of the text and open up the end of the novel to the increasing bewilderment of the reader. Which, we are bound to wonder, is the real ending to the story? Is it the matricide or the murder of Don Jesús? Is it Pascual's death as recounted by the chaplain and guard, or is it the transcriber's final rhetorical question, 'Qué más podría yo añadir a lo dicho por estos señores?' (p.165)? Is it intended to be rhetorical? The answer to the last question must surely be that a great deal more needs to be added to make the story both complete and fully intelligible.[6]

So far then, the documents have revealed a fundamental gap in the novel's structure, between its text and context. On one side of the gap we have a story of an individual in the past ending in matricide, on the other, a collective history in the present containing the shadowy outline of a revolutionary killing. The omission of the

---

[6]In the Biblioteca Nacional's copy of the first edition some wag has scribbled their own answer: 'nada, has dicho todo, gracias'.

latter is extremely effective because, as Giménez Frontín has perceptively stated, it creates a point of maximum tension in the novel and becomes 'el enigma central sobre el que gravitan toda una serie de retos interpretativos' (29, pp.31–33). Eventually we shall have to confront the question of why the gap is there, and the attendant problem of deciding which is more important, the matricide or the death of Don Jesús, and whether there is any connection between the two. At this stage, however, it is enough to note that the gap exists and that its presence crucially affects the various other contexts — narrative, moral, formal and historical — in which the novel is read and acquires meaning.

Let us take the narrative context first. To make sense of the story we need to know the point of view of the narrator. What exactly is the situation of Pascual Duarte while he is writing? From the covering letter we know he is inside Badajoz prison in February 1937. But what is he in prison for? To whom is he writing? Why is he writing? These three simple questions, which are basic to a proper understanding of what Pascual writes, cannot be answered with complete certainty, least of all by a first-time reader. Initial impressions would suggest that Pascual is in prison for the matricide, but, as we know, the dedication and the transcriber's second note point to imprisonment for the murder of Don Jesús. It would also be incorrect (71, p.135) to suppose (68, p.292) that Pascual is writing to Barrera López, the named recipient of his letter, because the person addressed as 'señor' and 'usted' in the manuscript is never named, and could only be identified as Barrera López if we took the letter to have been written before the manuscript, which presumably is not the case. And if one accepted Barrera López as the intended reader, it would be even odder (22, p.24) for Pascual to omit the one crime that would most interest the Count's friend in Mérida. It would be equally rash to assume that Pascual's purpose in writing is clearly defined by his reference in the same letter to a 'pública confesión' (p.15), for his opening sentence, 'Yo, señor, no soy malo, aunque no me faltarían motivos para serlo' (p.21), already suggests the opposite — an act of self-justification. An indication of the difficulty involved here is the variety of terms used to describe the manuscript. Pascual refers to it in his letter as a 'relato' and as 'esta especie de memorias' as well as a 'pública confesión', and in his dedication he calls it an 'escrito'. The term 'relato' is also used by the transcriber, who nevertheless seems to favour the term 'memorias', using it in both his notes. The preponderance therefore of more secular and neutral terms tends to weaken the idea of a confession. Even if we accept the text as a confession, our perception of its purpose is dependent on whether we regard the confession as primarily religious or judicial in nature. Is Pascual writing to cleanse his soul or save his neck?

Despite these confusions, the documents also offer clues to help clarify the situation. The first major breakthrough was made by Sobejano. From the prominence given to Don Jesús in Pascual's letter and dedication, he argues that the named recipient of the manuscript is a surrogate for Don Jesús: 'no es sino un "alter ego" del insigne patricio local. Es como si en la persona del Sr. Barrera López resucitase Pascual Duarte al Conde de Torremejía para explicarle, y explicarse a sí mismo, por qué todas sus violencias remataron en rematarle' (*66*, p.24). According to this, Pascual is really writing to Don Jesús in order to explain (presumably to the dead man's shade) why he killed him. However, an important modification has been made to this by Urrutia (*71*, pp.57–60). From the transcriber's clue about 'tinta morada' (p.159) — the purple ink suggests that the covering letter was written at the same time as Chapters 12 and 13 — and the reference in Chapter 6 to 'interrogatorios y visitas del defensor' (p.59), Urrutia argues that Pascual is writing to a judge in charge of his case, or the prison director, in order to appeal against the death sentence, and that this initial aim is later abandoned when Pascual retracts his appeal: 'no quiero pedir el indulto' (p.17). This helps considerably. But then Urrutia goes on to argue, too quickly, that once Pascual has confessed his guilt in Chapter 13 it no longer matters to whom he is writing, since his only aim now is one of self-explanation. This over-simplifies Pascual's purpose and minimizes the fact that the manuscript is ultimately sent as a 'ruego de perdón' (p.17) through

Barrera López to Don Jesús. If we accept that Pascual has been sentenced to death for the murder of Don Jesús, as we have to, then the figure of Don Jesús must loom very large indeed in Pascual's mind right up to the end. This is not necessarily inconsistent with the idea that he is writing throughout to someone in authority, to 'la muy alta persona a quien estas líneas van dirigidas' (p.34). If we take a later example in Chapter 17 where Pascual refers to 'este pobre yo, este desgraciado derrotado que tan poca compasión en usted y en la sociedad es capaz de provocar' (p.133), we can see that the 'usted' could still be any one of a number of people: Don Jesús, Barrera López, a judge, a higher authority, the general reader, even God (if the *señor* were capitalized), or someone else we cannot as yet identify. Whoever it is, the identity of the intended reader must have an important bearing on any attempt to decipher Pascual's purpose in writing. Indeed, the number of possible readers may suggest that Pascual's purpose is equally multiple, or variable, or extremely confused.

The problem of narrative point of view overlaps with the third major problem of moral response. This is because our judgement as to whether Pascual is good or bad (and whether he deserves capital punishment or not) is bound to be influenced by our understanding of his intentions as narrator, and this involves a decision as to whether he is being sincere, and whether his version of events is objective or subjective. First-person narrators are of course notoriously unreliable. In Pascual's case the problem of objectivity is compounded by doubts about his sincerity, as well as by the lack of a clear narrative context. But if we concentrate for a moment on the problem of objectivity, we see it, like most commentators, not as a problem of factual accuracy but rather as a question of moral objectivity: who is responsible for Pascual's behaviour, himself or others? Here our response echoes the standard debate in criminology over the causes of crime: personal or environmental, nature or nurture. Pascual anticipates the debate in his letter and resolves the issue by having it both ways, blaming himself and life in general: 'es demasiado lo malo que la vida me enseñó y mucha mi flaqueza para resistir al instinto' (p.17). One side of the debate was presented by Cela himself when in a 1960 prologue he blamed society: 'lo que se viene llamando el criminal no es más que la herramienta; el verdadero criminal es la sociedad que fabrica — o permite que se fabrique — la herramienta' (2, p.582). We should of course be wary of accepting Cela's later gloss as a reliable indicator of his earlier intention, even though it is often quoted as such (e.g. *18*, pp.133–34). The greatest objection to this social interpretation is to be found in Beck's more rigorous approach: 'un hombre "bueno" sencillamente no mata [...] Pascual matará brutalmente una y otra vez, pero con toda sinceridad tratará de convencernos de que no es un hombre malo' (*15*, p.288). Nevertheless, even though this is a pertinent hard-line to take, it begs precisely the questions already asked. Is it Pascual's aim to prove his innocence? Is he being sincere? Moreover, if his assessment of himself is not objective, is Beck's any more tenable? Does the axiom that killing anyone is wrong apply equally to the killing of Don Jesús, the matricide and Pascual's execution? Moral condemnation is also the line recommended against Pascual by the transcriber: 'Ves lo que hace? Pues hace lo contrario de lo que debiera' (p.14). But again what this assertion applies to is not clear. For like Beck's it appears to discount Pascual's present activity, including any attempt on his part to express remorse and explain the past. A more charitable attitude, which anticipates the softer line in Cela's later prologue, is taken by the prison chaplain. He listens to Pascual's confession and is convinced enough of its sincerity to conclude that beneath the brutal exterior ('una hiena') Pascual was really a gentle soul at heart, a lamb forced into violence by life, 'un manso cordero, acorralado y asustado por la vida' (pp.161–62). The hard-nosed prison guard, on the other hand, is less persuaded by Pascual's confession, regarding it as a symptom of mental illness: 'de la salud de su cabeza no daría yo fe aunque me ofreciesen Eldorado, porque tales cosas hacía que a las claras atestiguaba su enfermedad' (p.163). This, together with the guard's insistence on Pascual's cowardice, his 'miedo a la muerte' (p.165), ought to encourage a healthy scepticism about Pascual's motives and objectivity, both of which could be distorted by his state of mind or a desire to save his

own neck. When in the covering letter he apparently resigns himself
to the penalty of death — 'Ya ni pido perdón en esta vida' (p.17) —
we may wonder, along with Soldevila (*67*, p.111; and *38*,
pp.58–59), whether he is merely putting on a show of repentance in
an attempt to soften the hearts of the authorities and get a reprieve.
But even supposing it is a deliberate ploy, we need not regard it with
disapproval, because we might see it as an admirable stratagem for
Pascual to buy time in order to write down some form of protest in
the guise of a confession. We might also find the confession unreliable for another reason if we are led by Osuna (*53*; and *64*, p.273) to
suspect it may be the result of indoctrination, or more coercive
pressures exerted on Pascual by his jailers. In all of this the question
of Pascual's reliability hinges very much on how we evaluate his
narrative situation, and whether we think he is writing to the
authorities who control his earthly fate, or to a different and
posthumous readership. Some may feel I am over-emphasizing the
complexities of the situation, and may prefer to follow the guard and
put it all down to Pascual's deranged mental state. But instead of
simplifying matters, this would lead us to ask what it is that causes
the derangement or confusion. Indeed we should add this further
possibility to the whole picture, for it helps to define the limits
within which our moral responses are engaged. This is done by
extending the range of our dilemma from one familiar extreme — is
he good or bad? — to another — is he bad or mad? — (*15*, p.283),
while at the same time making room in between for a large area of
uncertainty, in which Pascual's confused, or conscious, role as
narrator may well be a deciding factor. The purpose of the
documents, then, is not to give clear moral guidance; it is, as Spires
argues (*68*, p.290), the systematic creation of moral doubt. Thus
they reinforce the ambivalence usually produced by Pascual's text:
we tend to sympathize with what he says, but recoil in horror from
what he does, before then going on to wonder what lies behind his
deeds and his words. Nor should we be distracted from Pascual's
words by taking the device of transcriber too literally and think, as
Spires does (*68*, pp.284–85; and *22*, pp.16–17), that the
transcriber's influence on the text is decisive. Whether used to

counter censorship or not, the transcription is a way of projecting and concealing the person who is ultimately responsible for the text, Cela himself.[7]

The fourth problem of interpretation is that of realism — the ways in which the novel makes reference to the wider context of reality. It overlaps with the previous problem of moral response in three respects. Firstly, Pascual's account of reality may be biased by his own self-assessment. Secondly, the novel's relation to the socio-historical background may distort the reader's own judgement, especially from an ideological viewpoint. Thirdly, the suspicion that Pascual may be mentally unstable could also undermine the reality of his account; for is there any evidence, other than Pascual's words, to exclude the possibility that the matricide, or any other event, is just pure fantasy or fabrication? Fortunately such a possibility looks remote because most readers will prefer to invoke the convention of realism and assume that Pascual's version of his life is, within the bounds of fiction, factually correct: the killings he describes did in fact, for the purposes of fiction, occur. How precisely the deaths of Lola and Don Jesús occur is of course a different matter. The more manageable issue here is to decide, on the one hand, how psychologically plausible and convincingly realistic is Pascual's story — Torrente Ballester thought it as amusingly fantastic as Peter Pan (cited *15*, p.280) — and, on the other, how accurately it reflects socio-historical reality, not just the way in which it portrays the life of a village in Estremadura prior to 1922, but also how it relates to events surrounding the narrator's situation in 1936 and 1937. Both aspects, the individual story and the wider history, are combined in the novel in an intriguing way by the presence of the textual lacuna, which marks a convenient separation between the realism of the story and the main references to its historical context, while at the same time bringing them into close juxtaposition. The lacuna highlights the problem of realism in both senses: firstly because the connection with history is obscured, and yet alluded to, by the

---

[7]According to Urrutia (*37*), in the original manuscript the transcriber's 'Otra nota', with its two letters, was added on and dated 7 January 1942. The first deleted) addressee of the letters was 'Sr. D. Camilo José Cela'.

omission of the last murder; and secondly because it indicates that the reality of Pascual's story is incomplete — it is not the whole truth. In fact the transcriber attaches to the lacuna the double issue of realism and historical reference when he says that 'la laguna que al final de sus días aparece no de otra forma que a base de cuento y de romance podría llenarse, solución que repugna a la veracidad de este libro' (p.159). The gap is offered as proof of the book's authentic reality as a historical document. But we know we are reading a work of fiction, and that the omission of a large chunk of the story may seriously diminish both the force of its realism and the scope of its reference. Moreover when the transcriber asserts that inventiveness (along the lines of a 'cuento' or 'romance') would not be a truthful means of completing the text, we have to take this with a pinch of salt, since the story bears some resemblance already to a tall story or ballad tale. Indeed the lacuna might appear to some as just one more implausible detail in a long string of implausibilities. We ought therefore to see the gap for what it really is: a literary device whose full meaning can be grasped only if we step outside the fictional frame of realism and study the frame of reference intended by the author, both the fictional author and the real one. Would either share the transcriber's distaste for fiction as a means of filling in the gap? We should remember that Pascual's initial letter invites us to use our imagination to complete the story: 'suspendo definitivamente el seguir escribiendo para dejar a su imaginación la reconstrucción de lo que me quede todavía de vida' (p.16). Admittedly he also implies there will be very little left to our imaginations. But this must be set against the enormous gap that is eventually left. To understand which way to take Pascual's invitation will depend on whether we think his ending is cunningly calculated or beyond his control. Obviously meant to be leading in this respect is the transcriber's information that Pascual 'preparó la carta con todo cálculo para que surtiese su efecto a su tiempo debido' (p.159). One can be misled into thinking that this means that Pascual is simply lying (*68*, p.286; *58*, p.924). But a more subtle interpretation would be that whatever gap is left at the end must enter into Pascual's calculations as narrator. And when the transcriber fills in the fact about Don Jesús, the real effect of this is not to curtail speculation, but to whet the reader's appetite for more details. Not only is curiosity aroused about the civil war context, we also find that the partial narrowing of this factual gap widens the semantic one between the matricide and the final murder, because they are so different. The omission of what Feldman rightly calls 'the most significant event in the novel' (*26*, p.658) is not only crucial (*22*, p.24), it leaves us relatively free to reconstruct that event for ourselves (*74*, p.43). Of course we have to use our knowledge of the historical context, but perhaps the main means of filling the gap is to use intelligently our imaginations. And the greater the gap appears to be, the greater the leap of the imagination required to bridge it; and correspondingly greater also is the problem of realism. In the transcriber's warning that to make this leap would spoil the 'veracidad' of the book, there is an interesting pointer to the convergence of the esthetic aspect of realism with its moral dimension. For implicit in his warning is the idea that speculation would be untruthful and dishonest. But on the other hand we might argue that if the gap appears to be of great significance, we should be less than honest not to try and explore it, even though the effort is bound to be subjective. To stimulate the reader to make the effort is, I believe, the intention which can be reasonably attributed to the real and the fictional authors, though many critics would certainly disagree with this.

One reason for the continued appeal of Cela's book among academics is the interesting way it exploits the problematic nature of the novel form itself.[8] And it is precisely the gap between text and contextual documents that has caused the biggest problem and led to the sharp polarization among the critics. This polarization is most noticeable over the question of realism, and takes the form of a

---

[8]For the traditional importance of these questions, see Graham Hough, *An Essay on Criticism* (London: Duckworth, 1966). On point of view and unreliable narrators, see Wayne C. Booth, *The Rhetoric of Fiction* (Chicago: Univ. Press, 1961). For textual gaps and indeterminacies, see Jonathan Culler, *On Deconstruction* (London: Routledge & Kegan Paul, 1983), pp.36–37. The title of my fifth chapter echoes Frank Kermode, *The Sense of an Ending* (London: Oxford Univ. Press, 1967).

divide between social and ontological approaches (*70*, p.165; *68*, p.283).

On one side, those who emphasize the socio-historical reality of the context have obviously not been deterred by the transcriber from trying to complete the story with varying degrees of imaginative guesswork. On the other side, those who emphasize the individual, existential, reality of Pascual's text have virtuously refrained from engaging in socio-historical speculation. But the irony is that the latter group, in their attempts to stick to what is objectively in the text, have often ended up imprisoned within the subjective confines of Pascual's story, unable to see it from a more objective historical context. (e.g. *35*, p.74; and *70*, p.175).

Critics are also sharply divided over their moral response to Pascual's character, and often in a way that coincides with the division over realism. The more emphasis there is on history, the greater the inclination to excuse Pascual for his actions. And vice-versa: the more the emphasis is on the story, the greater the tendency is to blame Pascual himself. This at least is the pattern set by the two most pioneering articles written so far on the work. Beck dismisses thoughts about Don Jesús's murder as pure conjecture (*15*, p.288), and sticks instead to the story, stressing the irony between Pascual's actions and words. Sobejano, on the other hand, combines a more sympathetic reading of Pascual's story with a crucial emphasis on its historical context, and does so by proposing a metaphorical relation of one to the other: 'la familia de Pascual Duarte no es sólo la familia carnal, sino la familia social [...]' (*66*, p.31). Sobejano is certainly right to say that any interpretation that excludes the historical context is bound to be incomplete (*66*, p.40). But his own interpretation of that context is also open to question, especially for those who like to remind us that Cela fought for Franco in the civil war and published his first novel in a blaze of Falangist publicity.

According to Cela's own account (*2*, pp.550–76) he wrote most of the novel while working in Madrid as a clerk at the Textile Syndicate in 1940–41. After some initial difficulties in finding an outlet the first edition was eventually published by Aldecoa in

December 1942. Its instant success soon led to a second edition, which was almost sold out when it was banned by the censors in November 1943. This attracted even more attention abroad, and the work was quickly translated into Italian and then English. After two years of censorship, during which a third Spanish edition appeared in Argentina, the publication of a fourth edition was allowed in Spain in May 1946, with a prologue by Marañón. For the first edition Cela had asked Baroja to write a prologue, but Baroja, quite understandably, said he did not want to be thrown into jail. Cela had to be content with just a wrapper on the second edition quoting Baroja's praise of the work as 'una novela, muy buena'. Probably more important for the novel's initial success was the backing from the Falange-dominated press, in particular from its head Juan Aparicio, who had apparently decided to promote the 26-year-old Cela as part of a Falangist literary renaissance, and presumably encouraged some reviewers to defend the novel against the disapproval of more conservative and religious sectors in Franco's Spain. The most detailed account so far of Aparicio's support, the early reception, and the little that is known of Cela's role during and after the civil war, is provided by Urrutia (*71*, pp.23–26, 35–52). He sees praise of the so-called virility of the novel's style as an attempt to associate Cela with a Falangist cult of violence (*71*, pp.45, 50–51), but instead of confirming and lamenting that association as Marfany tries to do,[9] Urrutia describes Cela's ideology in vaguer, less confusing terms as a kind of 'apartidismo liberal' (*71*, p.25), but without quite defining its application to the novel.

The precise relevance of this right-wing historical context has received its clearest and most critical statement from Osuna, who argues that, far from being a form of left-wing social protest, the novel mirrored the Nationalist cause because it situates Pascual's criminality in pre-civil war, Republican, Spain, whilst attributing his spiritual redemption to the new Spain inaugurated by Franco's

---

[9]The novel is said to be 'un magnífic exemple d'aqueixa ideologia nacionalista, irracionalista i vitalista' (*9*, p.43), a view echoed by Barry Jordan and Enric Sullà Alvarez, 'A Survey of the Postwar Spanish Novel. I, 1939–1954', *Vida Hispánica*, 30, no.1 (Winter 1981), p.19.

forces. The conflicting reactions of the censors could, according to
Osuna, correspond to three possible interpretations of its political
message. First it might have been seen as counter-revolutionary (a
permissible portrayal of the criminal Left), then as pro-revolutionary
(the criminal's biased account causes the novel to be banned), and
eventually as positively pro-Nationalist (the revolutionary confesses
his error, the old regime is repudiated, and the ban can be lifted)
(*53*, pp.93–94). Although this strikes me as a good argument for the
novel's political ambiguity, Osuna insists that the third and final
reaction he attributes to the censors is the one that most accurately
reflects Cela's intention — to censor for himself the socio-political
motives behind Pascual's last murder and thus, by omission, distort
historical truth (*53*, pp.87–88).

Urrutia however argues that the omitted murder has no political or artistic significance at all, for three reasons: firstly he claims
it cannot be dated precisely to the start of the civil war; secondly, it
is, he thinks, absent from Pascual's text (*71*, pp.62–67, 117); and
thirdly, if Cela had wanted to depict a revolutionary crime there
would have been no problem with the censor because of the
contrition expressed (*71*, pp.64–65). Nevertheless, Urrutia's own
quotation (*71*, pp.35–36) of the Head of Propaganda's outraged
letter in 1946 would appear to confirm both Osuna's emphasis on
the real difficulties (*53*, p.91) and Giménez Frontín's amazement
that the novel could get by the censors at all (*29*, p.33).

The main tendency among critics like Osuna who paint Cela
with a Falangist brush is to regard the omission of the last crime as
wilful self-censorship, and a serious defect on artistic and moral
grounds. Sanz Villanueva, for example, argues that any textual
connection with the civil war is too vague and ambiguous to be
meaningful (*63*, p.264); and he links this historical evasiveness with
Cela's support for Franco, as a reminder of which he cites Cela's
rather unsavoury letter of application for employment as an
informer with the secret police in 1938, based on his experience in
Republican Madrid in the first year of the civil war (*63*, p.250; but
see *22*, p.21).[10] Sanz Villanueva also criticizes the novel on artistic

---

[10]The letter, dated 30 March 1938, 'II Año Triunfal', is quoted in full (*29*,

grounds, for what he says are 'no pocos defectos formales' and 'una falta de decisión organizativa' (*63*, pp.258, 255). Thus, whilst recognizing its importance in post-war Spanish literature, he raises a question mark against the novel and minimizes the significance of the omitted crime.

Apart from censorship and Cela's integrity, there is another, even simpler, explanation for the final gap, one which reinforces the idea of defective composition. Reviewing Urrutia's edition (*4*) in *Anales de Literatura Contemporánea*, (1984), 365–66, Joaquín Rico Consuelo recalls Cela's own account of how he fell gravely ill towards the end of 1941 when the novel was still unfinished ('Mi novela estaba no sé si ya casi terminada o aun por su mitad, o poco más'), and wrote the letters from the prison chaplain and guard to bring it to an end ('para poner punto final'). Cela adds that he wanted to round the novel off as best he could ('Quería dejar la cosa un poco redondeada') in order not to leave behind his manuscript as no more than a 'triste e inútil recuerdo familiar' (*2*, p.551). This would seem to obviate the need for a complicated explanation based on either an internal reading of the text or external constraints such as censorship, and threatens to undermine any artistic significance that might be attached to the ending of the story as we have it. But since it is not clear where exactly Cela had got to when illness intervened, we cannot tell whether further episodes, if written, would have come before or after the matricide. Nor can we conclude that illness caused the Don Jesús episode to be omitted, for Cela's account does not exclude the possibility of conscious artistic choice. After all, if he had time to write the last two letters he could have included something on the final killing; and even after his recovery, and before the novel's eventual publication at the end of 1942, he still chose not to add any more details. What seems to me significant in this account is that rather than foreclosing debate about the ending, it offers instead some external support for thinking that

pp.46–47) and reproduced in facsimile (*11*, between pp.544–45). The 21-year-old Cela writes: 'el Glorioso Movimiento Nacional se produjo estando el solicitante en Madrid, de donde se pasó con fecha 5 de Octubre de 1937, y que por lo mismo cree conocer la actuación de determinados individuos'.

there emerges in the course of the narrative an important convergence between protagonist and author, and that both, when faced
with imminent death, make a literary virtue out of mortal necessity.

So the gap and its civil war connection remains a crucial
aspect. For Buckley it is, like Lazarillo's, the '"caso" clave' of the
whole novel (*19*, p.98). For Giménez Frontín it is a master-stroke,
'tal vez, el más feliz hallazgo estructural de la obra' (*29*, p.33). The
casual and ambiguous way in which the gap is presented can
certainly cause it to be ignored or dismissed (*18*, pp.124–25). There
is also the opposite danger of trying to read too much into the
ending. Indeed the questions of censorship, integrity and illness are
enough to put us on our guard. However, my own sympathies are
with Sobejano's positive appraisal of the effect created by the
omission of the last crime, the absence of which is rendered artistically conspicuous by Cela's use of a 'procedimiento alusivo-evasivo'
(*66*, pp.41–42). But an important part of the resulting effect has
been left unexplored by Sobejano as well as later critics, and this is
the extent to which Pascual as narrator is the one who censors
himself and so becomes responsible artistically for the final gap in
his story. It is only by concentrating more on the mind and character
of Pascual as narrator that we can find, I suggest, the best way to
appreciate the lacuna, and bridge the gap between story and history,
text and context, character and author, and between one set of
critics and the other.

Such then is the ultimate aim of this Guide. So far we have
looked at the main problems of interpretation posed by the novel's
most unusual and contentious feature, its appended documents. The
rest of the Guide will concentrate on other areas of particular
difficulty and importance. The gap or discrepancy that emerges in
Pascual's character in Chapter 1 is the subject of my next chapter.
My third chapter takes the study of his character a stage further
through an analysis of his story in the past. My fourth chapter looks
at the development of Pascual's character as narrator in the present,
focusing especially on the narrative crisis marked by the gap
between Chapters 12 and 13, which is, arguably, the turning-point
of the whole novel. My fifth chapter deals with Chapter 19 and

especially its relation to the ending, the final gap in the text. My Conclusion will try and define the intentions of both narrator and author as a way of drawing together possible solutions to the four main problems which have been raised in this Introduction. The views of other critics will continue to be mentioned, but the solutions proposed will be both tentative and mostly my own. I shall also continue to favour Pascual's Christian name over his surname, not just because of brevity (for it would be preferable to use Pascual Duarte throughout), but also because it acknowledges a certain sympathy in my own approach towards a novel which, like many great works, puts the reader on first-name terms with its central character.

2. Initial Problems (Chapter 1)

Chapter 1 is important because it immediately raises in a chillingly unexpected fashion the problem of understanding Pascual's character and of making an appropriate moral response to it. No reader can fail to be shocked by the abruptness of the change — in mid-sentence — from Pascual the subtle presenter and happy member of his village to Pascual the mindless killer of his own dog. By exposing the two sides to Pascual's Jekyll-and-Hyde character, the first chapter marks the extremes of sensitivity and barbarity between which his behaviour swings, and thus strikes a jarring discord that will reverberate throughout the story.

Besides the disturbing split in his character, Chapter 1 also exposes an obvious contradiction between the brutality of the shooting and Pascual's opening assertion that he is not bad — 'no soy malo' — or lacking reasons for being bad — 'aunque no me faltarían motivos para serlo'(p. 21). For clearly the killing of Chispa is indefensible, and its wickedness is made worse by the fact that it appears totally gratuitous. Pascual seems unable to understand his own motives, and his recollection of the event, though vivid, is limited to a few physical sensations (mainly heat) and visual impressions (the dog's stare), and their very intensity blocks out all other explanatory circumstances apart from what he now imagines to be a look of accusation on the dog's face. To do such a thing Pascual must be bad, or mad, or possibly both. It reveals what Entrambasaguas calls a 'monstruosa mentalidad infrahumana' (*3*, p.582). The disturbing discrepancy between Pascual's words and deeds has been most strongly emphasized by Beck. She regards his obvious lack of self-control, and the contrast between the impassioned nature of the killing and the apparent indifference with which it is described, without remorse or justification (*15*, p.290; and *68*, pp.299–300), as evidence for doubting his protestations of innocence. Whether there is no remorse or attempt at justification on his part may, as we shall see, be open to debate. But we can agree with Beck that the principal effect of the Chispa episode is to shake the reader's faith in Pascual's credibility as narrator: not only does he appear morally unreliable, his character in the present as well as in the past looks distinctly unstable; indeed so unstable as to invite a diagnosis of psychosis or schizophrenia (*66*, p.40). His fear of Chispa's stare, for example, has been described as schizoid (*41*, p.97). But does the psychosis, if such it be, still persist in the present, and if it does, to what extent is it only intermittent? For the crudity of the shooting and Pascual's inability to explain his motives are all the more disturbing in contrast to the subtle, articulate, and sane way in which most of the first chapter is written.

The opening two paragraphs in particular are remarkably sophisticated in the way they voice a muted protest against social inequalities using words and phrases that echo a more conservative philosophy (cf. *68*, pp.285–86; *18*, pp.35–37). The first paragraph starts off paying lip service to the idea that all men share the same mortal destiny, and recalls the allegory of the two paths which traditionally depict the moral divide between those who follow the hard path of virtue and those who follow the easy path of vice. Except that here the images are twisted round to convey a different message of social division: men are divided by birth into two classes, the privileged who enjoy an easy life along the 'camino de las flores', and the underprivileged who have a rough time of it along the 'camino de los cardos' (p.21). According to Catholic tradition, each man is free to choose between the paths of good and evil. Pascual however implies that moral differences are the product not of free will but of social conditions and birth, with the result that the rich are virtuous ('inocente') whilst the poor are vicious like wild animals ('como las alimañas') (*64*, p.266). In the words of the critic who has best analysed the initial description of Pascual's village, the first paragraph reveals 'un sentimiento de diferencia social no por envuelto en la superstición fatalista del hombre rústico menos evidente' (*66*, pp.29–30; *71*, pp.134–38). And, as Sobejano also points out, among the images Pascual uses to convey the general idea of a socially and morally divided humanity, there are some which have a much more local application. Images of the rough life ('cardos', 'chumberas', 'sol violento' and 'llanura') refer quite specifically to Pascual's geographical environment in Estremadura; and images of the easy life ('flores' and 'sonríen') are noticeably adjacent to the flowers in Don Jesús's garden and the smile on his face in the dedication. The possibility of this particular allusion is of course unlikely to occur to a first-time reader. Hindsight and a close re-reading, indeed, are necessary to grasp what Pascual is implying even in a more general way; that is, that the underprivileged are scarred for life with 'tatuajes' by their circumstances and are forced to behave violently to survive: 'arrugan el ceño como las alimañas por defenderse'. In other words, social deprivation denies the privilege of moral choice and provokes violent resentment. The question we are faced with in this first chapter is to what extent this opening proposition is applicable to Pascual himself, and especially to the brutal killing of Chispa.

In the second paragraph the focus shifts away from general divisions to a particular division between Pascual and 'usted', the anonymous reader. The resentment felt by Pascual is again softened by the use of a traditional framework, the cradle to grave symmetry provided by the first and last words 'nací' and 'muerte', and by the rhetorical cadence of the repeated phrase 'lisa y larga'. The latter by its repetition makes a subtle connection between a life of poverty and hunger ('sin pan') and the criminal behaviour which presumably has led to the condemned cell, whilst at the same time it insinuates that the reader's good fortune ('para su bien') prevents him even imagining Pascual's situation, either in the present, behind bars, or in the past, enduring poverty.

Potential ambiguity arising from the radical message of resentment and its philosophically resigned expression would appear to be averted by Pascual's combative opening sentence, the purpose of which seems clear enough: he is not a bad person by nature, though he is forced into bad behaviour by circumstances. Yet there is a hint of contradiction here: on the one hand he asserts he is not bad, but on the other hand, perhaps he is bad, even though he has reasons for being so. The additional ambiguity latent in the tenses used ('soy' and 'faltarían') only surfaces as a remote way out of the difficulty by restricting Pascual's claim to the immediate present (*60*, p.70); though one assumes they include his past nature as well as present. In order for the opening assertion to be convincing, the reasons, or 'motivos', for the killing of Chispa (in the past) must be demonstrated. But as we see, there are no immediately obvious reasons for the crime. And to compound matters, the socially deprived background that might provide a possible reason does not seem sufficiently adverse to prevent Pascual from adapting happily to it. The confusion encourages readers to follow the lead of Sobejano (*66*) in thinking that the description of Pascual's background implies at an ironic level much more and worse than it says.

On the surface Pascual remembers the details of his house and village with affection and even pride. This mood is in part explicable as a lyrical glow of nostalgia generated by Pascual's situation in the condemned cell. But it must also correspond, presumably, to moments in the past of genuine happiness. This would explain his willingness to accept social divisions of property as part of the natural order of things, as when he says that in his village 'como es natural, había casas buenas y casas malas' (p.22) and describes his own house as 'estrecha y de un solo piso, como correspondía a mi posición' (p.23). However, beneath the surface there are other implications. The contrast between Don Jesús's imposing residence in the main square and Pascual's humble abode on the outskirts points to a sharply divided social structure; in Sobejano's words, 'las clases sociales aparecen así distinguidas breve pero netamente: el pueblo pobre al margen y pegado a la tierra; la nobleza y la iglesia en el centro, realzadas' (*66*, p.27). The existence of this social divide is further underlined by certain details which, although fondly recollected, are also ironic. Take for example Lola's joke about the eels Pascual catches in the stinking stream by their back door. Behind the fact that they were fattened on the food that Don Jesús had eaten the day before, there lies the far from amusing reality of insanitary housing conditions: Pascual's hovel is situated downstream on the receiving end of Don Jesús' sewage; one critic even sees this as the reason for the Count's murder (*3*, p.585). Problems of water supply are also glimpsed in the references to Pascual's contaminated well and the dried-up public fountain, both of them in marked contrast to the private abundance of water which Don Jesús is able to lavish on his flowers. A further contrast is also discernible between the clock on the town-hall that never works and the alarm-clock in Pascual's home that always does work, 'como Dios manda' (p.24) (*66*, p.50). Social inequalities are of course only implied in these details since Pascual makes no explicit protest about them. He does so, however, when he moves from the specific to the more general, remembers the lights of Almendralejo visible in the distance, and complains about the ignorance of rural reality by city folk: 'Los habitantes de las ciudades viven de espaldas a la verdad' (p.27). The general divide between town and country thus reinforces the complaint about different social categories made in the opening two paragraphs, and may point to a similar way of interpreting Pascual's message. Just as the initial cliché of all men are mortal but not all are moral is undermined by the complaint that not all men are equal, so the description of Pascual's village may set up a further cliché of the poor but happy peasant, knowing his place within, at the bottom, and on the margins of society, only to subvert the rosy picture through the subtle accumulation of details which indicate a far from idyllic reality, in fact one of clear social injustice, since it can be concluded that 'mientras don Jesús lo tiene todo, Pascual no tiene nada' (*62*, p.68). Other details which Pascual fondly recollects, such as the smell of his stable and his prowess at fishing and hunting, serve to reinforce the impression of adaptability and contentment; but again, on reflection, they can be read ironically as further signs of social deprivation, in the form of primitive living quarters and a cultural preference for the violence of hunting over the more peaceful activity of fishing. If there is irony here, it may well arise from the fact that Pascual is trying to do two different and perhaps incompatible things: prove that he is not a bad person by demonstrating his ability to adapt to his role in society (*15*, p.289), and at the same time show that on other occasions he has reasons, such as adverse circumstances, for behaving badly.

Where the argument, and the balancing act, break down, of course, is in the description of Pascual's relationship with the hunting dog Chispa. Even those who are not dog lovers cannot fail to be perplexed by the sudden change from affection to aggression. Shooting the bitch seems to demonstrate precisely what Pascual seeks to deny — his capacity for evil, for unjustified and unmotivated violence. And yet, might the breakdown here be due simply to Pascual's poor presentation of his case? If there is meant to be a cause and effect relationship between the shooting of Chispa and the social background, Pascual fails to help the reader see the necessary connections, even though, in the second of the opening paragraphs, Pascual says he knows that the reader is unable to imagine the kind of environment Pascual has endured. Indeed the fortunate reader, both fictional and real, may well be so much in ignorance of the kind of life lived by Pascual as to be truly incapable of judging whether the killing of Chispa is gratuitous or provoked, psychotic or socially conditioned, atypical or typical. As Cela's 1960 prologue says, 'No es fácil aplicar la norma a lo anormal' (2, p.581). And even if it can reasonably be described as abnormal (how many peasants kill their own dog like Pascual does?) it could still be argued that a certain percentage of violent and psychotic behaviour is predictable and inevitable in conditions of social deprivation, especially in the case of a tiny minority who are exposed to stress and have a low tolerance factor, as a sociologist might put it.

But that is precisely what is missing from Chapter 1: not only is there no apparent reason, there is no evidence of the kind of stress that could explain the unmotivated killing of Chispa. Because the causal link is so tenuous, the wary reader, faced with the dilemma of judging Pascual's action, is bound to retort that the brutal and cowardly murder of an innocent animal, especially a favourite pet, can only be regarded, at best, as a caricature of a defensive reaction against adversity, and, at worst, as a grotesque example of 'kicking the dog', taking it out on something else in the heat of the moment. But without knowing what 'it' might be or the context of the moment, the brutal shooting, given the starkness of its presentation, seems out of all proportion to any environmental cause, whatever that might be. Pascual, one can argue, may be a case of poor impulse control aggravated by his background and breeding, but that is to lean over backwards — as Champeau does (*22*, pp.32–33) — to understand and excuse him. Given the contrast between the sophisticated and morally articulate writer of the opening paragraphs and the person scarcely able to articulate his feelings or thoughts at the end, sceptical readers, like Beck, are bound to smell a rat and reject Pascual's implicit proposition as untenable. It is hard to see the killing, in all its sickening crudity, as anything other than a violently psychotic act, one which rips apart the delicately composed portrait of home and village life, with its subtly insinuated divisions, to reveal instead a personality that appears to be itself pathologically divided. So, for the conscientious reader, the most worrying division becomes not so much the one in Pascual's village as the one exposed to view within his character.

The main dilemma facing us, then, is the lack of any coherent connection between the two sides of Pascual's character: the happily adjusted and articulate person on the one hand, and on the other, the mindless killer. Some sort of intervening process would be necessary to understand Pascual's sudden lurch into violence and to bridge the gap between the stark alternatives of either a sociological or a psychopathological explanation. Glimpses of this process might be found in the ironic signs of negative conditioning I mentioned before: Pascual's preference for hunting over fishing and his attachment to the smell of the stable, which strikes Beck as particularly ominous (*15*, p.289). Another clue might be his disorientation on a visit to the city — with the curiously anticipatory phrases, 'como un perro de caza', 'la sangre me calentaba todo el cuerpo' and 'como una piedra' (p.26) — together with the reassurance he gets from the familiar odour on his trousers. This might suggest that the primitive conditions to which Pascual adapts may also restrict his capacity to cope when circumstances change. But we are clutching at straws. In Chapter 1 we know there are no signs of changed circumstances or any increase in stress. Except, that is, for the brief passing mention of a change in Pascual's mood towards his favourite stone on the day he kills Chispa: 'y hubo un día que debió parecerme tan triste por mi marcha[...]' (p.28). This detail is equally tiny but it can, and has been, linked to a later clue.

Our main difficulty in understanding the Chispa killing comes from the fact that it is narrated out of context. As several critics have noticed, the unscheduled live reappearance of Chispa in Chapter 10, at a moment during Lola's second pregnancy when Chispa has just had a litter of still-born pups, gives us a glimpse of what might have been the proper context. Sobejano (*66*, p.25) relocates the killing to Chapter 11, after the death of Pascualillo, and explains it psychologically as Pascual's way of dealing with the accusations he receives and the guilt he feels over the marriage's failure to produce viable offspring. This explanation was first offered by Feldman (*26*, p.657) and is now the most accepted one (*44*, p.34; *46*, p.113; *69*, pp.43, 45; *38*, p.52; *18*, p.83). The relocation of the shooting to Chapter 10 itself (*26*; *44*; *38*) provides perhaps the more precise context, since it contains three references to the look on the bitch's face (p.86), echoing the obsessive insistence — six times — on the same feature immediately prior to the shooting, and shows Pascual in a state of 'tensión', 'agobio' and 'pena' (pp.85–86), which in turn echoes the sadness he saw projected onto his favourite stone in Chapter 1. Pascual in Chapter 10 is distraught, even out of his mind, with the possibility that Lola may have a second miscarriage — 'La idea de que mi mujer pudiera volver a abortar era algo que me sacaba de quicio' (pp.85–86); and this coincides with a change in Pascual's attitude to his dog — 'la Chispa — que por entonces viva andaba todavía — parecía que me miraba menos cariñosa' (p.86). We are surely right therefore to see a clear association between the bitch, the wife's miscarriage, and Pascual's feelings of guilt about his own childlessness. He realizes in the course of narrating the shooting that the look on Chispa's face was a look of accusation: 'ahora me doy cuenta de que tenía la mirada de los confesores, escrutadora y fría' (p.28). It is reasonable then to suppose that the physical agitation and sensation of heat that overcomes Pascual at the end of Chapter 1 is provoked by an intense feeling of guilt, and that this triggers the violent discharge of emotion onto the dog at a time when Pascual was obviously overwrought and not in complete control of his faculties. Ilie's (35, p.53) attempt to make a direct causal connection with Pascual's guilty, because unmanly, affection for his favourite stone fails to convince precisely because it ignores the later context. Nevertheless, Ilie's analysis has the virtue of emphasizing an important link between the shooting and what will emerge as a central feature of Pascual's character: his virility complex or fear of appearing effeminate, especially his fear of not being man enough to produce healthy offspring. This we shall return to later.

The more immediate issue is to determine what effects are produced by our realization that the Chispa episode is chronologically out of context. What is the significance of the narrative dislocation? When this goes unnoticed the killing appears only gratuitous (23, p.128), perhaps even the most unjustifiable of all the crimes (52, p.115). But, as Sobejano rightly says (66, p.25), when restored to the later context (whether Chapter 11 or 10), it becomes much less gratuitous and more comprehensible, though not necessarily any more justifiable. Sobejano is well aware that the killing of Chispa appears on the surface to be the unmotivated act of a psychopath without necessarily deserving the criticism and ironic reading insisted on by Beck. The restoration of the crime to an identifiable family context allows Sobejano to preserve some connection between Pascual's personal problem and society at large. Indeed the narrative displacement of the shooting from the family situation to the wider social context of Chapter 1 would also encourage Sobejano's view that society is a logical extension of the family. Yet there is nothing to stop us thinking that the movement of displacement goes in the other direction instead (or as well): out of the social background of Chapter 1 into the later family situation of Chapter 10, thus weakening the former in favour of the latter. This would also strengthen our first impression that the family and social contexts are quite separate, both from each other and from Pascual's action, and serve only to distract our attention away from what the narrative dislocation immediately highlights: seen in isolation the killing is an act of unmotivated, incomprehensible, aggression. In support of this view it must be emphasized that Sobejano's interpretive procedure can only be carried out retrospectively, and cannot erase the initial dreadful impact of the shooting for first-time readers, for a stylistic analysis of which see (*69,* pp.40–43; *68,* pp.299–300; *22,* p.36). The brutal impact of the killing is so discordant and remains bereft of any explanatory context for so long that it continues to disturb us throughout the book, especially when the lurch into violence is repeated again and again. The effects, therefore, are more complex than the approaches taken by either Beck or Sobejano would allow for. Sobejano tries to absorb the crude irony underlined by Beck with a subtle social irony, but the truth is that the contextless gap in which the shooting is placed opens up a space in which ironies and uncertainties proliferate to the discomfiture of readers, at least those who re-read to seek some explanation. Obviously this effect of discomfiture caused by the unreliability of the text and the instability of its context requires further analysis.

The narrative displacement has, I think, to be regarded as a deliberate device of discontinuity. When the chronological sequence breaks down, it exposes a gap between two contradictory views of Pascual's character, and forces the reader to flounder about in search of a coherent explanation to close the gap. Does the disordered narrative reflect Pascual's mental disorder in both the past and the present, or is it a symptom of social disorder? Which is the most compelling context for making sense of the killing: the later family context, the wider social context, or the lack of any context that isolates the action as a purely personal and pathological problem? Deciding any of this is difficult enough, but the problem is compounded by a question which none of the critics so far have ventured to raise: who, or what, is responsible for the narrative dislocation? Is it evidence of Pascual's crude mental derangement, or Cela's subtle textual arrangement? Can it be seen as a deliberate device employed consciously by Pascual as well as by Cela? Both Beck and Sobejano assume, in common with most other critics, that Pascual is not fully in control of his narrative. For Beck the Chispa episode must seem an obvious blunder on Pascual's part: he is

unaware that it contradicts his initial claim to be good (*15*, p.290).
For Sobejano it must seem a symptom of the mental pathology that
prevents Pascual from sharing the author's full ironic awareness of
the social background to his behaviour (*66*, p.31).[11]

There is some foundation for thinking that Pascual is not fully
in control from what he says himself at the beginning of Chapter 5
(p.45). There he apologizes for 'el poco orden que llevo en el relato'
and explains that he is not structuring his story chronologically
'como una novela', but instead he is following the order in which he
remembers people in his life, which makes him jump backwards
and forwards in time — 'por eso de seguir por la persona y no por el
tiempo me hace andar saltando del principio al fin y del fin a los
principios como langosta vareada'. There is, I suggest, more to this
than meets the eye (particularly behind the seemingly generic
'persona'), but at least on the surface it appears to confirm that the
narrative sequence is to some extent determined by the vagaries of
Pascual's memory and the people and things that are on his mind at
any particular moment. In fact, however, the narrative is neither the
series of portraits nor the stream of consciousness that might be
inferred from this, for it follows a fairly chronological order of
events, with this one exception, the killing of Chispa. What Pascual
could be referring to also is the constant oscillation of his text
between events in the past and what he is thinking in the present.
This later passage, then, does not tell us whether Pascual is responsible for placing the Chispa episode where it is; instead it begs again
the question of whether his actions as narrator are as naive as he
makes out.

In any of these cases there must be an ironic divergence
between Pascual's narrative order and the author's intended
meaning. Before we come to the possibility of a convergence
between Pascual's intentions and the author's order, there is

---

[11]I am applying to this specific instance Sobejano's general comment:
'aunque Pascual Duarte obra a menudo como un demente […], creo que, no
tanto en la conciencia de Pascual Duarte cuanto en la de su hacedor, está
presente, por vía de alusión y reticencia, la validez de Pascual como el
destino de una gran parte del pueblo español' (*66*, p.31).

another, less satisfactory, way of interpreting the narrative disorder, unconnected with either Pascual's personality or Cela's hidden intent, and that is to follow Spires in attributing ultimate and arbitrary control of the narrative to a transcriber who manipulates Pascual's already disordered and unnumbered manuscript (*68*, pp.285–86). This consideration is for certain sections of the text a feasible but unnecessary reading, for it ignores the transcriber's function as an authorial disguise and passes the buck of interpretation. Urrutia likewise asks who has decided the narrative order, and suggests that even if the transcriber could theoretically be responsible for the order of chapters, the sequence of events within each chapter must be Pascual's (*71*, pp.117–18), except perhaps where Spires detects the presence of the transcriber's editing, such as ellipses indicated by dotted lines. But in the case of the Chispa episode it is hardly possible to see where a break in the manuscript might be situated. The transition to the shooting occurs, as we know, in mid-sentence; the event is therefore firmly embedded in the narrative context of Chapter 1. So we still have to consider the intentions of Pascual and Cela, not the transcriber's.

I should like to explore five possible ways of interpreting the displacement of the Chispa episode. Their order follows a graduated scale (from simple to complex) of what I think is objectively discernible in the text. Although I have revised the number and order slightly to correspond to the five interpretations of the ending I shall propose in Chapter 5, I hope I am not imposing too subjective a model of coherence on the material that arises from the complicated interaction between an unstable text and a reader who, as Champeau rightly says (*22*, p.18), cannot afford to be passive.

(i) We can hypothesize that the chronological dislocation is caused by the vagaries of memory already mentioned, with the assumption that Pascual is naively unaware of the effects of his narrative on the reader. Like Beck, we can insist that Pascual has blundered, unable to see that the Chispa crime must be his responsibility and contradicts his initial claim not to be bad; since it cannot possibly be justified, it proves he is bad. Or possibly mad, since the absence of a context for the killing of Chispa, carried out in the

intense heat of the moment, might be a basis for a plea of
diminished responsibility, both for the past action and the present
narration of it — mindless violence mindlessly narrated. For what is
clearly pathologically disturbed behaviour there may also be
circumstances such as social injustice and family stress that
contribute to it, if we can, like Sobejano, do what Pascual seemingly
cannot, and that is make an explicit connection with the earlier and
later contexts. Nevertheless, narrative disorder in this interpretation
would remain primarily a question of Pascual's psychological
disorder.

(ii) Or we can think that Pascual is fully aware of what he
narrates, and that the dislocation forms a coherent part of his self-
defence as an example of the demented violence which, although it
may seem gratuitous and psychotic on the surface, is nevertheless
traceable to the later family context of distress (Chapter 10), which
in turn is only explicable in the wider context of social deprivation
insinuated during the first, sophisticated, half of Chapter 1. The
narrative dislocation might then be seen as an equally sophisticated,
pseudo-naive, strategy. Pascual might even conceivably be
pandering to the reader's prejudiced image of him as a crazed killer
by presenting his worst side, confident that it can still be excused by
implying that he is not to blame if he cannot control his violent
impulses: it is because his upbringing (and whatever the *usted*
represents) have not given him the means to do so. The narrative
disorder would be a conscious, though covert, challenge to the
established order of society that causes but cannot comprehend
abnormal behaviour (Cela's prologue hints at a similar parallel
between social and narrative orders, p.9).

(iii) A third possibility is to regard the dislocation as a
deliberate confession of guilt by a Pascual who chooses to introduce
the killing at the start as an example of his past wickedness. This
would not necessarily contradict the opening assertion of 'no soy
malo', since the confession of past crimes would permit the
repentant sinner in the present to prove himself to be not so bad
after all, especially when he can also show some extenuating
circumstances ('motivos para serlo'). Though 'no soy malo' sounds

initially more like a justification of the past than a possible defence against a charge of incorrigible evil (meriting death and damnation), we should remember that in his narrative of the killing Pascual uses an image of confession — 'ahora me doy cuenta de que tenía la mirada de los confesores, escrutadora y fría, como dicen que es la de los linces' (p.28) — which may not just indicate Pascual's incipient realization of what happened with Chispa, but also allude to his present situation in the condemned cell. Do we detect behind the image of 'confesores' the pressures he may be under, either to make a full confession and gain absolution, or to appeal against the sentence of those to whom he has already confessed his crimes? We might incidentally wonder if the image of 'linces', like the other previously quoted one of a 'langosta vareada' (locust beaten with a stick), betrays a confession made, and being made, under duress. Whether the confession is sincere or enforced, this interpretation would see it as a fully conscious one, with Pascual being aware of the two explanatory contexts for the killing of Chispa, but discounting them and detaching the crime from any context that might speciously justify it. The narrative disorder would then be a conscious recognition that the killing constitutes a sinful departure from the natural order.

(iv) Or we can follow the tendency of those who emphasize Pascual's narrative as a form of self-discovery, a therapeutic way of confronting what is bad and mad in his own character. The sudden eruption in Chapter 1 of the Chispa episode could be seen as a semi-conscious blunder, the surfacing of a mixture of aggression and guilt, a confused awareness both of his tendency to hit out at others (including here the dog and the reader) and of the shame he feels at doing so. To some extent Pascual is in control of the process because he allows this episode to intrude and stand ambiguously as it is, with no obvious context, thus dramatizing his own confusion, but also his growing awareness ('ahora me doy cuenta [...]') that his slaughter of the dog can only undermine the initial aim of self-justification. So here the emphasis shifts from the external contexts to an internal context, the mind of the narrator; and the narrative disorder becomes a means of expressing and curing the narrator's own psychological disorder.

(v) A fifth and final possibility is to regard Pascual as completely in control of his narrative and fully conscious of the literary effects of contradiction and ambiguity created by his deliberately dislocated narrative. Not only would he be articulating his own inner conflict, he would be presenting the killing of Chispa in such a way as to make it resonate with multiple meanings as a symbolic anticipation of later violence. The context here becomes more artistic; and the narrative disorder more expressive of a wider disorder. It is no longer just a question of whether Pascual is good, bad or mad: it is also a matter of turning a bad action and an apparently bad (defective) narrative to good effect, in both a moral and esthetic sense.

These five possibilities show that a close reading of this part of the novel (like many other parts) can involve us in complex, even convoluted, problems of interpretation, usually created, or aggravated, by the ambiguity of the context and the uncertain purpose of Pascual's narrative. We have just seen how the opening sentence of the manuscript ('no soy malo'), which appears to declare a clear purpose, becomes less and less clear the more we consider it in relation to the implicit context of the narrator and to the explicit context in the narrative, where the episode it introduces (the killing of Chispa) reflects back on it the various possibilities of meaning outlined above.

The majority of critics would prefer, I imagine, to steer a middle course between, on the one hand, taking too simplistic a view of the matter, or on the other, embracing the deconstructionist dogma that all meaning is multiple and unfixed, with no one meaning 'privileged' over any other. Some meanings, I believe, are preferable to others; the difficulty is demonstrating why. In this case, through the very dislocation of the narrative that unfixes meaning, the reader is forced to complete this part of the text by supplying and weighing the contexts that seem most appropriate. Of the five interpretations of the context outlined above, the last one is for me the best because it is the most complete, capable of containing all the others. Nevertheless, I am in some doubt as to whether

Pascual has yet reached that stage of artistic convergence with the hidden author. He may still be in the growing stage of confused self-awareness denoted by (iv).

Conscientious re-readers should still be in a quandary. Whichever author we take to be responsible for the dislocation, Pascual or Cela, it does not completely solve our difficulties. Neither the intended meaning or the acquired meaning of the Chispa killing can be established with absolute certainty. Without firm guidance from narrator or author, we are left to flounder among several, often incompatible, possibilities. But at least they can be defined. Even though Foster may be partly right to say that 'all attempts at explanation are only conjecture' (27, p.28), he is wrong to belittle conjecture. The text forces us into conjecture and provides several contexts to guide our guesswork. Perhaps, therefore, the fundamental significance of Chispa's death is to highlight the problem of explaining violence, by raising it in the very first chapter, and then, by omitting the explicit context and supplying two implied contexts (social and family), to demonstrate how easy it can be to jump to conclusions (Pascual's problem is a social one, a family one or a purely personal one; he is good, bad or mad) and how difficult it is to get at the truth of the matter, especially if we try to relate one context to another, as well as taking into account the intentions of the narrator and author, which are in turn dependent on their respective external contexts.

Several critics have ventured some other definitions of Chispa's symbolic significance.[12] The favourite one is to link the bitch with motherhood, firstly and fairly convincingly, as we have seen, with Lola's pregnancy, and then more remotely and less convincingly with Pascual's mother (*69*, p.45; *49*, p.63; *50*, p.51). Even though the mother is compared to a 'perra parida' (p.51) and, like Chispa, stares accusingly at Pascual (pp.100, 102), it seems wrong to limit Chispa's significance to the mother. Equally feasible, and equally remote, would be a link in Pascual's mind with his

---

[12]Nobody has speculated on Chispa's name. Might it mean a literary event full of *chispa*, a witty play of meaning, or a spark igniting a firecracker of violence? Cela described the work as a 'petardo' (*15*, p.295).

father, who will die after being bitten by a rabid dog in Chapter 4 (*16*, p.315; *51*, p.217). Even more far-fetched, but just as feasible, and supported by Estirao's threat to shoot Pascual 'igual que a un perro rabioso' (p.130), would be an association of the bitch with Pascual himself, in the sense that because he kills other people (his mother, Don Jesús) in the same callous way that he kills Chispa, he will also be put down like a rabid dog. More to the point is Bernstein's idea that the Chispa episode is 'a model of the killings which ensue' because of its 'apparent lack of motivation' (*16*, p.315). Equally perceptively Champeau says the chronological disorder makes the incident emblematic. But of what? Despite revealing between Pascual and the dog an interesting pattern of trust and dialogue being replaced by silence and violence, she explains away the killing by seeing Pascual too simplistically as a victim of social alienation (*22*, pp.27–28, 32–33). To cover all these various possibilities, I suggest that Chispa's death not only foreshadows most of the violent episodes to come, it also anticipates the difficulty of assessing each one, including the matricide and the murder of Don Jesús, the specific contexts of which have likewise to be conjectured and reconstructed.

This last point is an extremely crucial one for underlining the literary function of the Chispa episode. Not only does it set up a pattern of violence in the novel's content, it also foreshadows future episodes whose narrative form is equally dislocated, creating a gap in the text that corresponds to a gap in our ability to make a coherent whole of either the text or its narrator. In the case of the final and most important gap in the text, when we find its artistic significance challenged by various circumstantial explanations (censorship, illness, etc., as I mentioned in my Introduction), then we can point to the very first chapter and show that narrative gaps and the problem of filling them are built into the novel's structure and the narrator's character right from the start. If Cela had to end the novel prematurely, he did it in a way that was consistent with a pattern already established in the narrative.

But even more important, the Chispa episode also offers possible procedures for attempting to bridge these gaps. We have seen how more sense can be made of the shooting if we follow up certain textual clues in order to reconstruct two things: the chronological context and the psychological context in which the incident took place and takes place. When future gaps occur in the text, the same process of reconstruction may well be necessary. Indeed this will be the case in the next chapter when we consider Pascual's character as it develops in the past. In order to understand his behaviour we shall find it useful to reconstruct the psychological pattern of his violence and its chronological arrangement.

3. Characterization in the Past

In the previous chapter we saw how the killing of Chispa could be placed in four different contexts: in isolation as an act of blind impulse, in a family situation of stress, in a wider and more abstract context of social and metaphysical injustice, and in the context of the narrator's present state of mind. I shall suggest in this and the next chapter that Pascual's behaviour can be analysed into a pattern consisting of four different levels which roughly correspond to those four contexts: a first level of impulsive unawareness, a second level of socio-cultural awareness (in which Pascual is conscious of his family honour and social reputation as a man), a third level of moral awareness (responding with love or hatred to what is perceived as just or unjust), and a fourth level of self-awareness (in which guilt and aggression are internalized). The first three levels are glimpsed in Sobejano's classification of Pascual's crimes into three categories: 'proceden, desde el automático impulso de desquite [...] pasando por la emocional venganza de honor [...] hasta llegar a una especie de venganza metafísica contra el origen de su vida desastrada' (66, pp.26–27). His analysis stops short of considering the possibility of a fourth level or a common denominator.

I shall argue that there is a central obsession which is common to all four levels and helps resolve the major problem of making sense out of Pascual's unstable and contradictory character. Although Alborg sees Pascual's characterization as unconvincing because it lacks psychological depth (13, p.84), Entrambasaguas stresses Pascual's pathological brutality whilst admiring the creation of an 'extraña y cuidada psicología'(3, pp.583, 581); and most critics have remarked on Pascual's unusual combination of savagery with both sensitivity and reflectiveness (1, p.xxv; 52, p.115; 63, pp.256–57). Brown best expresses the complexity when he says:

the novel's chief merit is its subtlety, in its revelation
that the violent peasant protagonist, outwardly brutal-
ised by a fatal chain of circumstances, is a tragically
complicated personality, struggling with the intolerable
psychological burdens of a genuine sensitivity, a
demanding and potentially noble moral conscience, and
a manifestly Oedipal relationship with his odious
mother [...] (*8*, p.145)

Some of the complication noted here arises from Pascual's role as
narrator in the present (which is the subject of the next chapter). But
already we find that his character in the past is complex enough to
have prompted a wide variety of responses, all of which have to deal
somehow with the fact that almost everything that is known of
Pascual comes from his first-person, and therefore subjective,
narrative. Indeed, a curious feature of the characterization, which
few critics even note (except *62*, p.52), is the absence of any
conventional description of Pascual's external physical appearance,
a lack emphasized by the chaplain's postscript regretting not being
able to supply the transcriber with a photograph (p.162). As a result
we are in direct and almost exclusive contact with Pascual's inner,
psychological, self, even though we gather from his actions that he
is a very physical person. The only clues to his appearance are the
chaplain's initial impression of him as a hyena (though this is
perhaps more moral than visual), Don Conrado's jest about 'esa
cara tan fea que tienes' (p.136), and the information that Pascual
worked in Corunna as a porter and a bouncer, all of which suggests
a strapping, course, even fearsome-looking peasant, an impresssion
which is supported by the violence of his actions and belied by the
sensitivity of his soul. So we have both a paradoxical character and
paradoxical characterization.

Gradually a more comprehensive picture of Pascual's inner
personality seems to be emerging, based on the solid, though
restrictive, foundations laid by Ilie's study of his primitively rural
mentality (*35*, pp.41–56). Ilie explains Pascual's violence

psychologically as the product of inarticulateness, irrationality, emotionalism, physicality and *machismo*. After discussing the various causes of violence suggested by Pascual himself (fate, sin, circumstances) Ilie finds them so confusing that for him the ultimate significance of the violence can only be esthetic and existential (*35*, pp.72–73), and so leaves unexplored important social and moral dimensions (as well as the crucial development of narrative articulacy). Nevertheless, what has proved perceptive and influential is Ilie's stress on Pascual's inability (in the past) to verbalize his emotions, and even more important its connection with Pascual's violent 'masculinismo' resulting from a basic insecurity about his manhood (*35*, pp.50–53). What Ilie and most others have curiously neglected is the fact that 'todo gira en torno a la obsesión que tiene Pascual de demostrar su hombría procreando hijos o, cuando fracasa, recurriendo a la violencia' (*34*, p.2). Pascual needs to prove his manhood to compensate for the acute inferiority complex that derives initially from his family background, and subsequently from his failure to produce a family of his own. What I have referred to as Pascual's 'machismo patológico' (*34*, p.2) and his 'complejo de virilidad, o de familia' revolves crucially around the turning-point of the whole story, the death of his child Pascualillo (*33*, pp.118–19). This obsession with paternity, also noted by Masoliver (*48*, pp.5–6), is not only at the centre of Pascual's character, it is arguably the principal factor uniting virtually all his violent outbursts. Lottini recognises its importance (*43*, pp.203, 206) but still regards it as subordinate to the linguistic impotence (*43*, p.195) emphasized by Ilie. Yet as Champeau says (*22*, p.24–30), Pascual's inarticulacy is not connected to social conditioning alone; for the most telling episode of linguistic impotence occurs when the mother blames him for Pascualillo's death. Indeed Champeau explains the matricide as Pascual's attempt to reassert the manhood that his mother's criticism has previously denied him. Since (as we shall see in a later chapter) the circumstances of the matricide are not made explicit except for Pascual's hatred, it could well be argued that all of Pascual's problems, including his pathological insecurity, stem from early childhood and a continuing absence of motherly love (*41*, pp.97–98; *50*, p.51), with the novel's central feature being, in Zamora Vicente's words, 'el odio del hijo no comprendido ni acariciado jamás' (*74*, p.29). This is clearly important, particularly in the case of the matricide, and has led Masoliver to follow Brown's cue and stress Pascual's maternal Oedipal complex, though in a loose and confused way (*48*, p.6; *49*, pp.59–60), without realizing that the Oedipus complex is both a mother and a father problem, and one which is too technical and too wide-ranging to be discussed here (see *34*). In any case, as Jerez-Farrán has demonstrated (*38*, pp.50–55), all of Pascual's violent actions are linked, not to the mother, but to masculine insecurity, and specifically to frustrated fatherhood. Jerez-Farrán thus brings out the psychological coherence of Pascual's violence, even though by concentrating on the socio-cultural conditioning of *machismo*, he minimizes the level of psychosis beneath it, and, above it, misses the moral and mental dimension of Pascual's hatred for his mother. Indeed this latter aspect, Pascual's moral judgmentalism, has been offered as the principal factor in all the crimes by Marban, who describes it as Pascual's primitive sense of justice (*46*, pp.129, 190) following Marañón's definition of Pascual as a 'juez elemental' meting out rough justice to everyone (*45*, p.11). In order to decide which aspects of Pascual's personality are most important, it will be helpful to take a closer look at his behaviour to see whether, beneath the chaotic alternation of violence and calm, there emerges a more significant pattern than a purely formal or emotional one (*71*, pp.119–24).

Most commentators are agreed that the main body of the novel, and with it the development of Pascual's character, falls into three distinct stages, separated in a clear and symmetrical way by Chapters 6 and 13, which interrupt the story of the past to describe the narrator's present situation in prison. The first stage in Chapters 1 to 5 covers Pascual's family background; the second stage in Chapters 7 to 12 dramatizes his attempts to create a family of his own; and the third stage in Chapters 14 to 19 shows how failure to do so leads to a total destruction of family life. The only major disturbance of the chronological order is, as we know, the transfer of the Chispa episode to the beginning. One result of this is to obscure from view the interesting fact (*66*, p.24) that of the seven violent crimes committed by Pascual, the first, chronologically speaking, is the knifing of Zacarías in Chapter 8, at the start of the second stage when Pascual is already a grown man, at least 28 or 30 years old (p.55). In other words his criminal violence is a relatively late development, and not the immediate consequence of social deprivation and a broken home. Pascual is neither the typical *pícaro* or the juvenile delinquent one is led to suppose by the literary echoes and the outburst of violence at the end of Chapter 1. There are certainly signs of emotional disturbance and chronic insecurity produced by his upbringing (with vivid descriptions of the drunkenly violent and loose-living parents and the grotesque deaths of the father and brother), but just as remarkable is Pascual's genuine desire to overcome his disadvantaged background and erase the social stigma attached to his parental home by creating a family of his own. This initial drive to conform, adapt and win respect should be given due emphasis (*44*, pp.36–37; *48*, pp.5–6).

Consequently, despite the killing of Chispa, the formation of his character in the first stage is one of real progress. This is demonstrated in the scene in the cemetery in Chapter 5, when he responds to Lola's provocative challenge and possesses her sexually after a fierce struggle right on top of the fresh grave of Mario the handicapped brother. Despite the sacrilegious aspect of this episode (which helped provoke the ecclesiastical ban on the first edition), and its primitive violence — Entrambasaguas describes it as 'puramente sexual, como un apareamiento de bestias' (*3*, p.583) — it nevertheless represents a moment of successful adaptation to village life. Because Mario is associated in both Pascual and Lola's mind with genetic abnormality, that is, lack of manhood (*35*, p.52), and because Pascual is obviously apprehensive about his physical ability to reproduce, it comes as a relief to him, and a real personal triumph, when Lola apparently applauds what for one critic is 'virtual rape' (*41*, p.98) by saying: '¡No eres como tu hermano!... ¡Eres un hombre!...' (p.58). The resulting pregnancy reassures

Pascual about his reproductive capacities, and he receives society's approval in Chapter 7 when his future mother-in-law promptly invites him to stay the night. Esthetically as well as morally, it seems to me that the act of defloration is legitimized by the image of poppies used to describe the drops of blood on Mario's grave from Lola's broken hymen; the 'media docena de amapolas para mi hermano muerto' (p.58) not only superimpose the idea of fertility on top of violence and death (*18*, p.75), they also touchingly symbolize the purging and redemption of all that is negative about the family background, the epitome of which is Mario's hideous existence.

So, for some time at least, the influence of family background on Pascual is not wholly negative. Indeed, the acute feeling of inferiority which it produces in Pascual stimulates his desire to win respect and adapt by conforming to social conventions of male behaviour and marriage (*18*, pp.148–49). Even the hatred Pascual comes to feel for his mother and father may be viewed as a healthy moral reaction against their bad example. Pascual's sister Rosario, though prostituting herself like her mother, does much to encourage the morally positive side of his character, since she is the only member of the family able to give a lead in showing love and being supportive on crucial occasions, such as when she picks the injured Mario up off the floor at the end of Chapter 4. Hints of an incestuous relationship with the sister are, in my opinion, misleading (*16*, p.302). Pascual's bad side, on the other hand, is encouraged by the parents' behaviour. What he especially loathes in his mother is her lack of feeling, her callous indifference to suffering, some of which he admits has rubbed off on himself; 'porque a nada se odia con más intensos bríos que a aquello a que uno se parece y uno llega a aborrecer el parecido' (p.53). Pascual's hatred contains a good deal of self-hate, traceable perhaps to his inferiority complex. And like his father, who beats his wife and is then captivated by Rosario, Pascual develops a similar tendency to lurch between extremes of violence and tenderness, strength and weakness. Although he seems, for the moment, to be able to adapt to adversity better than his parents — 'procuraba conformarme con lo que me había tocado, que era la única manera de no desesperar' (p.32) — Pascual fears he has inherited their worst defects, namely, their irrationality and lack of self-control, their inability either to 'pensar los principios' or 'refrenar los instintos' (p.31). Pascual must have absorbed standards of decency from somewhere to be able to react against his parents, but his capacity to do so is not helped by the nature he inherits or the very limited nurture he receives by way of parental example and formal education, having left school early with the active connivance of his mother.

A brief survey of the formation of Pascual's character in the first stage of his story shows a potentiality for both good and evil, and the question is finely balanced as to whether his behaviour will be negatively conditioned by his upbringing or whether he can overcome it in a positive way. The Chispa episode, as we know, already points to a negative answer. But at the outset of stage two of the story everything seems to depend on whether Pascual can adjust by creating a successful family life of his own. The failure to do so, following the death of his son Pascualillo in Chapter 10, will be dramatically underlined by another reference to the handicapped brother when Lola cruelly rubs salt in the wound and accuses Pascual of being physically defective like Mario: '¡Eres como tu hermano!' (p.99) (22, p.30). So the central drama of Pascual's family life helps to bring out what is the basic dynamic in his character: the need to compensate for an acute sense of social and genetic inferiority by proving himself a man in the eyes of the rest of the village. At first this virility complex takes the conventionally constructive form of marriage and a desire to father children; when the desire is frustrated, it seeks an outlet in an increasingly antisocial and destructive fashion. The main issue then facing us will be to decide what, or who, is ultimately responsible for Pascual's failure to cope with misfortune and the subsequent degeneration of his life into multiple murder. Is he at fault, or other people? Is it fate or society? Whatever the answer is, other questions hover in the background: why is Pascual's success or failure measured only by his reproductive capacity? Is this due to cultural limitations or individual psychosis? Does the same standard of measurement continue to operate in the second marriage?

Before considering the main issue, I wish to return to the curiously regular pattern that I suggest is discernible in Pascual's career of violence. In the first stage the initial outburst against Chispa is compensated for to some extent by the deflowering of Lola. The process outlined in Chapter 1 of a regression from sophisticated moral and social awareness to blind impulsive aggression is happily reversed in Chapter 5 when Pascual's aggressive impulse is channelled into the more constructive outlet of sexual impregnation, which, as we know, receives in Chapter 7 the blessing of others and is sanctified by the church. In other words, with Lola, Pascual manages to coordinate the different levels of his personality in a positive way that enables him to be fully integrated into his local community. Thus, for a short time at least until the fight with Zacarías, the marriage to Lola dispels the ominous impression of a highly disturbed personality, isolated from others, which was created by the psychotic outburst against Chispa. Looking back at this incident, it is interesting now to detect erotic undertones in the description of Pascual's gun, his 'escopeta, de un solo caño', which 'se dejaba acariciar, lentamente, entre mis piernas' (p.28). He experiences the same rush of blood to the head when looked at by the bitch as he does later when confronted by Lola's accusing stare in the cemetery, the essential difference being that in the later incident Pascual is able to respond positively and keep his aggression under control and subordinated to his sexual impulse. With Lola Pascual asserts his manhood in a violently primitive but socially acceptable way.

In the intervening chapters of the first stage, the violent streak in Pascual's character is either inhibited or just developing, and is activated not at the level of primitive instinct, as with Chispa and Lola, but at the other two levels already mentioned. The second socio-cultural one involving male honour comes into play in the first verbal confrontation with Estirao in Chapter 3. It is also reflected in Pascual's fear of appearing effeminate — 'blando' (p.50) — when he thinks of picking up Mario, and in his angry reaction to two phrases which he imagines to be further implied slurs on his manliness: the priest Don Manuel's flattering description of him as 'una rosa en un estercolero' (p.47), and Señor Rafael's insinuating repetition, after the death of Mario, of the old phrase of consolation, '¡Angelitos al cielo!' (pp.54–55). The third, moral, level is applicable to Pascual's hate for his mother, which, as he makes clear in Chapter 5, is not born out of impulse — 'que ni el amor ni el odio fueran cosa de un día' (p.53) — but is the gradual development of a conscious moral awareness of her failings. The fact that Pascual situates the moment when she turns into an 'enemigo rabioso' (p.53) within the period when she remains unmoved by Mario's death, suggests the feeling of hatred for her is by association (through Pascual's apprehensive identification with Mario's abnormality) also linked to Pascual's obsession with his manhood. So the connection is there long before the virility complex and hatred for the mother become obviously connected at the end of Chapter 12, and again, less obviously, in Chapter 19 when he blames her for the problems besetting the later marriage (22, pp.30, 34).

In the second, middle, stage Pascual begins to translate his latent aggression into action. He knifes Zacarías (Chapter 8), kills the mare (Chapter 9), shoots Chispa (Chapter 10?), and goes almost to the brink of murdering his mother (Chapter 12). This last incident involves not only the emotion of hate but also doubts about whether hate can justify killing, and corresponds therefore to what I have called the moral level of Pascual's character. The death of the mare clearly belongs to the irrational level of impulse, just like the shooting of Chispa, except that in the case of the mare the mingling of sexual impulses with the discharge of aggression is more explicit, while the situation itself, immediately following Lola's miscarriage, clarifies the psychological process taking place: sexual-paternal desire is frustrated and displaced as aggression onto the animal used as a scapegoat. The knifing of Zacarías in a drunken brawl on Pascual's return from his honeymoon, would appear to take place at a purely impulsive level; but the cause of Pascual's anger is Zacarías' joke about a 'palomo ladrón' (p.78), a phrase which Pascual understands as yet another slur on his manhood. It may take extensive dictionary research for the reader to find that 'palomo

ladrón' can refer to a cock pigeon that entices hen pigeons away
from their mates. Jerez-Farrán's idea that Zacarías is calling
Pascual a thief weakens his otherwise lucid discussion of the episode
(*38*, pp.50–51). Whether the over-sensitive Pascual reads too much
into the allusion is uncertain; but what is clear is that the cause of
the fight (the implied threat to Pascual's brand-new marital honour
through Lola's potential infidelity) places his violent reaction on
what I have called the second, socio-cultural, level.

The same curious pattern is repeated, with a vengeance, in the
final third of the story. Lola dies in Chapter 15 possibly of fright
and a heart attack according to some (*15*, p.294; *16*, p.309; *44*, p.34;
43, p.211), but I think it more realistic, given her strong constitution
and Pascual's track record, to presume, or at least suspect, along
with others (*56*, p.268; *27*, p.17; *38*, p.53), that he has his usual
sudden rush of blood to the head and strangles her. Though the
reason is marital dishonour, and though Alborg thinks it unconvincing (*13*, p.86), the way Lola's death is obliquely narrated puts it on
the same pathological level as the killings of Chispa and the mare,
as a regression to blind unconscious impulse. The cause of Pascual's
dishonour, Estirao, is the next victim (Chapter 16). When Pascual
kills him, he is this time fully conscious of his action as a graduated
response to Estirao's increasingly provocative insults. Whether one
judges this manslaughter as justified (*74*, p.41), cowardly (*15*,
p.295) or implausible (*13*, p.87), the socio-cultural level of male
honour is clearly the overriding factor here. When the crescendo of
violence culminates in the premeditated murder of the mother
(Chapter 19), we find that the decision to kill her is taken at a much
more abstract level, dominated by the idea that hatred of evil makes
killing both justifiable and inevitable. In other words, here the
moral and intellectual level is uppermost, even though to bring
himself to do the deed Pascual has to regress down through the
other two levels, first the social one in which Pascual's pride is at
stake — 'Era ya una cuestión de amor propio' (p.153) — and finally
the primitive level of unconscious impulse, with a familiar mixture
of aggression and erotic undertones. Chapter 19 curiously reflects
back on the episodes in Chapters 1 and 5. It is almost a mirror

image of the same regression through three levels which ends in the shooting of Chispa, with the crucial difference that the matricide is a fully conscious and coordinated action. Despite Brown noticing 'the same passionately ambivalent mood' (*8*, p.145), it is also an image in reverse of the intercourse with Lola, with the difference here that in the matricide all three levels of Pascual's character point in a morally destructive direction: instead of sex, honour and love with Lola, Pascual experiences a lethal combination of hatred, shame and aggression towards his mother.

If my perception of this symmetrical pattern of behaviour is correct, it is still difficult to grasp what its significance might be. The three-tier classification suggests that, even though Pascual's levels of aggressive behaviour are all linked coherently to the central obsession with virility and paternity, they also create a complex three-dimensional problem of assessing the violence, involving issues of psychopathology at level one, social anthropology at level two, and moral philosphy at level three. Our judgement of Pascual is further complicated by other considerations. At the level of blind impulse, where his character is at its most unstable and his victims are at their most innocent, it is nevertheless possible to make a plea of diminished responsiblity. At the second level there are strongly extenuating socio-cultural circumstances, involving honour and extreme provocation, hence the leniency of the prison sentence following the manslaughter of Estirao (28 years reduced to 3). If Lola was indeed strangled, the legal vacuum following uxoricide could easily be explained by the socio-cultural acceptability of an act carried out in the heat of passion, with diminished responsibility, and in response to a clear case of marital infidelity, even though we might agree that Pascual provoked it by leaving home (*15*, pp.294–95). And at the third level, where Pascual is most responsible for his actions and at his most coldly calculating, he also feels most justified in what he does. The premeditated killing of his mother, which for some (*26*, p.657; *74*, p.41) is the only real murder committed, nevertheless presumably had sufficient grounds for the defence to merit a life sentence rather than the death penalty. To condemn Pascual outright (*3*; *15*) or to exonerate him completely

(*74*; *66*; and *18*, pp.117–19) is to evade many of these complicating factors. It is difficult to escape the dilemma first posed by Chapter 1: is society or psychosis to blame, is Pascual deprived or depraved, is he good, or is he bad? Is he mad? Does he drive the reader mad? Indeed one can sympathize with the reaction of Jerez-Farrán when, after leaning over backwards to understand the socio-cultural conditioning of Pascual's violence, he decides in the end that Pascual is a thorough rogue who makes excuse after excuse for what is inexcusable. However, those who condemn Pascual outright tend to forget that he comes to hold himself partly responsible, or at least, like many readers, he becomes genuinely confused about what proportion of blame is to be allotted to himself or to factors beyond his control.

This confusion is clarified to some extent by the arrangement of the story into three distinct stages, each one of which, I suggest, highlights in turn the three main explanations or emphases favoured by critics: society, fate, Pascual's own faults. My analysis of these stages will use the three levels of behaviour already discussed, and also a favourite recurring image of Pascual's, that of the *camino,* in order to pinpoint at every stage what Beck suggests is the central moral and philosophical issue of the novel: a conflict of free will and determinism, choice versus destiny (*15*, p.285). The first stage, beginning with Chispa's death and ending with Lola's virtual rape, emphasizes above all the problem of Pascual's impulses, both sexual and aggressive. Can they be controlled and channelled with or without the help of social conditioning? The opening of Chapter 1 with the two *caminos* suggest that there is no moral choice: the ability to control impulses and the direction in which they are channelled depends entirely on family environment and birth. But it has not been sufficiently noted that the outcome of the first stage suggests the contrary: moral choice is possible, and Pascual has successfully chosen a virtuous path of social adaptation, proof of which is the integration of his personality achieved in his success with Lola, in marked contrast, as we saw, to the disintegrated character who kills Chispa. If we look again at the original statement of the problem in Pascual's first sentence — the conflict between good nature ('no soy malo') and bad nurture ('aunque no me faltarían motivos para serlo') — instead of being undermined by the Chispa episode (which seems to indicate bad nature), that statement still remains valid by the end of the first stage: Pascual's nature can overcome poor nurture, particularly if his good side receives positive reinforcement outside the home. Of course this brief period of adaptation and self-esteem is extremely fragile. Pascual may have emerged relatively unscathed from his grotesque family environment, but the killing of Chispa has already indicated the formation of a psychotically flawed personality. Even if we can perceive behind the hyena who shoots his own dog the young man who is a gentle lamb at heart (to use the chaplain's imagery), already at the beginning of the second stage, whether by foresight or hindsight, Pascual is apprehensive of success, and views his approaching marriage to Lola with the same fatalism as a lamb being taken to slaughter (p.70). Is Pascual right to see himself as a helpless victim, or will he help to bring disaster on himself? Free will or fate?

The central event and turning-point of the middle stage is the tragic death of Pascualillo in Chapter 10. The eleven-month old child succumbs to a 'mal aire traidor' (pp.90 and 92), some sort of chill or infection, perhaps not an altogether abnormal occurrence in the conditions of third-world poverty and infant mortality prevailing in remote Estremadura in the early part of this century. Pascual's wife and mother take it understandably as a tragedy, but irrationally hold Pascual responsible because he appears in their superstitious minds to be cursed by God — 'maldito' (pp.100–01). This idea of predestination and a malevolent fate is echoed by Pascual at the beginning of the next chapter: '¡Quién sabe si no sería que estaba escrito en la divina memoria que la desgracia había de ser mi único camino, la única senda por la que mis tristes días habían de discurrir!' (p.93). The *camino* image here has significantly narrowed down Pascual's options in life to one predestined course of disaster. This, we must remember, is confirmed only retrospectively; as an explanation it depends on an irrational belief in the decree of a god (Latin *fatum*), and fate of course as a catch-all explanation for tragedy may be a cover-up for personal failings or social flaws, and as such has been used by some (*21*) even more enthusiastically and less critically than Pascual himself. At this point Pascual's idea of fate is shaped by religion and centres on God's punishment of sins committed, or still to be committed. But leaving aside the question of divine injustice, it is clearly unfair of Pascual's mother and wife to blame him for being genetically incapable of producing strong healthy children. Without further information in the text about possibly poor parenting or social conditions that might help explain more rationally this particular infant's death, one can only conclude that it is due to misfortune, a pure accident of fate (in a secular sense). But the second crucial factor in this middle stage is Pascual's subsequent inability to cope with this misfortune, an inability which, it must be noted despite Beck's strictures (*15*, p.293), is considerably aggravated by the lack of support from wife and mother, and by the pressures arising from the socio-cultural emphasis on procreation. Faced again with frustration and failure as a father, Pascual reacts to criticism with guilt, anger and hatred. But the violence that erupted previously against the mare and bitch, now at the end of Chapter 12 stops just short of murdering either wife or mother — note the plural '¡Porque os he de matar!' (p.100) — as Pascual leaves the village and runs away from both the problem and his own violence. Hindsight not only leads Pascual to see himself as a victim of fate, he also sees himself as responsible for choosing the wrong course of action, and admits that running away was a disastrous move to make: 'mi huida, mi mayor pecado, el que nunca debí cometer y el que Dios quiso castigar quién sabe si hasta con crueldad' (p.118). For Pascual to suggest that this was a worse sin than killing may seem preposterous. But it also shows his openness to the issue of choice versus inevitability: he is now able to see how he contributed to his own downfall and made things far worse by running away.

Nevertheless, the central event of this middle section is still the death of his baby son, which highlights the basic cause of failure as one of pure misfortune. Just as the effects of social environment on Pascual's impulses was the main issue in the first stage, here, in the second stage, at the risk of drawing too neat a pattern of correlation, what is most prominent is the second, socio-cultural, level of his personality, suggesting that his success or failure in acquiring self-esteem and social respectability turns on a trick of fate, pure chance, the child's unfortunate chill. Displaced into the background, but not entirely lost from view, is the nature/nurture debate, which is touched on when we wonder whether Pascual lacks the strength of character to cope, or whether more family and social support would have helped him cope better. Fate undoubtedly takes priority as an explanation in this middle section, but it is subtly questioned by the alternative explanations of society and self, just as the overwhelming effects of society in the first stage were modified by the competing notions of fate and free will.

The third stage of the story begins with Pascual on the road: 'comencé a caminar — sin saber demasiado a dónde ir' (p.110). Like the picaresque *golfos* and Galician peasants he meets, he attempts the traditional route of seeking better fortune by migrating. But after two years away he stubbornly returns in the naive hope that things will be better at home, only to find Lola pregnant by Estirao. Pascual now appears trapped in a vicious circle, doomed to an escalating cycle of hope, frustration and violence. In Chapter 17, on returning from his reduced term in prison for the murder of Estirao, Pascual blames fate, 'esa fatalidad, esa mala estrella' (p.132), and also society for his predicament, for making him a 'desgraciado derrotado' (p.133). But these two explanations, carried over from the first two stages of his life, are seriously qualified by the irony of the situation, irony of ironies says Beck (*15*, p.296): instead of an adverse fate and a hostile society, good fortune and a seemingly compassionate system have rewarded his good behaviour with early release, albeit at a time when he is still unable to cope with other people's behaviour. In almost the same breath as he blames fate and society, he recognizes his own measure of responsibility, his 'muchas culpas', and 'penitencias' (p.134) for what he has done. Indeed any emphasis on the hostility of fate or society would seem to be undermined altogether by Chapter 18 where Pascual is given renewed hope, and another chance, through his marriage to the appropriately named Esperanza. So in the last Chapter when the mother is seen as the main reason for the troubles arising in the new marriage, the central issue has to be re-stated in its fullest form: does the mother represent the forces of society, fate, and other people that determine Pascual's violence; is she the victim of his personal problem, the projection onto her of his own psychotic self; or is her murder a conscious, even valid, attempt to change his destiny of his own free will?

The issue of free will is implicit in other recurrences of the *camino* motif. The apparent inevitability of failure is seen in Chapter 17 when Pascual returns home from prison with renewed optimism only to be reminded, as if by Providence, of his past misfortunes, just as he walks by the village cemetery situated midway between the station and his home, 'hacia la mitad del camino' (p.139). The inescapable shadow of the past is clearly emphasized at this point, though the possiblity of choosing to keep a steadfast route into the future might be glimpsed in the picture of his shadow flitting between the path and the cemetery wall, 'ora tirando recta por el camino, ora subiéndose a la tapia del cemente-rio', a possibility soon to be presented of course through Esperanza. Likewise two more *camino* images, used just before the beginning and then at the end of this third stage, appear to convey an over-whelming sense of foreboding and disaster: 'dar un empujón a estas memorias para ponerlas en el camino del fin' (p.107), and 'iba indefectiblemente camino de la ruina' (p.155). But the impression of inevitable doom is both superficial and deceptive. The first of these two examples in fact expresses Pascual's decision in Chapter 13 to begin writing the concluding part of his story; and the context of the second reveals that it is the road to ruination that he is trying to avoid by carrying out the decision to kill his mother. So a careful look at these three later uses of the *camino* image serves to reflect what is the main emphasis on the agency behind events in this third stage: not fate but Pascual it is who is actively involved in choosing his course of action, either positively by returning home in Chapters 14 and 17 in the hope of erasing past failures, or negatively when he reacts with violence to the provocations of Lola, Estirao and finally his mother. In other words Pascual is the active and reactive agent, he tries to shape his own destiny by taking violent justice into his own hands. And, as the culminating act of matricide confirms, the level of his character which finally predominates is the third level of moral awareness. In this third stage, the principal issue is no longer simply one of good or bad upbringing, or one of good fortune or bad: it is a struggle between what Pascual perceives as morally good (himself) and evil (others). So he reacts murderously to the provocations of those who stain his honour and ruin his dreams of a happy family life. His violent over-reactions constitute of course his main character defect, but it is no longer just a question of impulse (Lola) or honour (Estirao): the matricide is a conscious, premeditated, and morally self-justified action. It is this major factor that is added by the third stage to the cumulative process of depicting and explaining the course of Pascual's life: to social determinism (first stage) and predestination by fate (second stage) is added Pascual's self-determination (third stage).

It seems to me that Pascual's character and story in the past can be properly analysed into the three levels of behaviour and the three distinct stages outlined above. Moreover, no level or stage supersedes another; they all accumulate to form a complex picture of one individual's career of violence. What remains uncertain is the extent to which the three behavioural levels are highlighted by each stage in a neatly configured pattern, such as the one I now offer as a summary. The first stage explores how far Pascual's impulses are conditioned by social and family environment; the second stage shows how his socio-cultural role is determined by fate/fortune; and the third stage reveals how much his fate/fortune is determined by his conscious recourse to violence. At each stage and level the same basic question arises: does Pascual choose his own path in life, or is it chosen for him, by the society in which he is born and bred, by fate, or by others? I do not have a simple answer to this question, nor can I pick out easily any of the factors highlighted at each stage as being more important than the others. Most critics however have tended to prefer one or other of these possible explanations. The vast majority have seen society as the decisive factor (*23*, p.129; *66*, pp.32–34; *46*, p.77; *47*, pp.93–94; *55*, p.365; *22*, p.32; and *18*, p.133). Several have emphasized fate (*1*, p.xxv; *21*); others have pointed the finger at Pascual himself (*3*; *15*; *48*); one says both fate and self (*62*, p.38), and another the conflict between fate and self (*26*, pp.656–57). We might accept Cela's 1960 statement that Pascual is the product of society (*18*, pp.133–34), despite his other 1960 statement that his way of thinking had changed since 1940 (p.9). Equally we might prefer his lesser known assertion that *fatum* has an important role (*2*, p.592; *14*, p.31); or his declarations about man's essential wickedness (*18*, p.154). Even though Cela seems never to have stated that Pascual in particular is wicked, we could quote the novel itself to support the third possibility that Pascual is responsible for what he does. But as I have suggested, the text of the novel can be used to support all these varying approaches. Livingstone has stressed the complexity of the issue by referring to the 'fine balancing of individual responsibility and the force of destiny' and by defining Pascual as a 'self-willed victim of fate' (*41*, pp.99). Like Livingstone many of us find it hard to decide whether Pascual is the gentle lamb who is forced to become a hyena (as the chaplain claims), or a person who lets himself become a cowardly and vicious predator, despite his early assertion that man has no choice over his fate: 'como no nos es dado escoger, sino que ya — y aun antes de nacer — estamos destinados unos a un lado y otros a otro' (p.32). Even here in a passage that apparently rejects the notion of free will, Pascual is choosing (trying) to make the best of his lot in life: 'procuraba conformarme con lo que me había tocado' (p.32). His room for manoeuvre is of course grotesquely limited, but at each stage of his story we see him exercising some degree of choice: he responds to Lola's challenge and chooses to marry her; at the end of Chapter 12 he chooses to restrain his aggression and leave instead; in Chapter 19 he chooses this time to stay and kill. Looking back Pascual can still remember all the pressures of upbringing, misfortune, and other people's behaviour, that forced him to make those choices, but he also begins to grasp the fact that there might have been other alternatives: Esperanza, we learn (p.145), fancied Pascual even before he married Lola (she might have made a better wife); he could have stayed at the end of Chapter 12 and coped with the situation, or, once gone, he could have stayed away for good; and did he really have no other choice but to kill his mother (*15*, p.297)? The complexity of his character is thus increased by the insight he gains into both himself and the external forces that controlled his past life. For it is only now when seeking to justify these murders that he comes to realize the choices he made were the wrong ones, as he openly admits in his covering letter, using once again the significant image of the *camino*: 'Pesaroso estoy ahora de haber equivocado mi camino' (p.17). This guilty self-awareness takes us onto the fourth level of his personality and the fourth stage of the story, which are the subject of the next chapter.

Before that I would like to draw attention to another even more important theme (that of children) which, like the *camino* motif, serves to underline the four different levels of behaviour and stages of the narrative. The wretched existence of Mario illustrates the worst aspects of the background, both genetic and environ-mental, that shapes Pascual's own character and exposes Mario to death by drowning in a vat of oil. Even though another *camino* image ironically suggests the choice of suicide on Mario's part — '¡Bien sabe Dios que acertó con el camino [...]!' (p.48) — it is obvious that he had neither a choice or a chance. Pascual does, but are they as restricted as his brother's short existence seems to indicate? Pascual probably thinks so, and even seems to imply in the ironic attribution of suicide to Mario that this might have been the best option for himself (*17*, p.78). But in fact the first stage ends with Pascual trying to create a new life on top of both Mario's grave and Lola. In the middle stage, as we have seen, the life and death of Pascualillo highlight dramatically the accidents of fate on which the father's fortune or misfortune depends. In the third stage the child motif seems to disappear, though we are reminded that the cemetery in Chapter 17 contains the remains of Pascualillo and Lola's miscarried foetus. Since we are not told whether Pascual has any children with his second wife Esperanza, this absence of children in the third stage underlines the emptiness and failure of Pascual's family life. But hidden almost from view in Chapter 14 the motif continues because Lola is pregnant with Estirao's child. The double death of mother and embryo, directly caused by Pascual (or indirectly if we want to give him the benefit of the doubt), emphasizes his more active and violent role in determining his existence. To sum up: Pascual is a victim of his social background like Mario, a victim of fate like Pascualillo, and like Lola's embryonic child he is a victim of people, including Pascual himself. We shall see in the next chapter how the image of the child is a significant detail also in the fourth and final phase of his characterization. When his life is most constricted by imminent death in the condemned cell, writing will give him a last chance to exercise free will and create something that will outlive his struggle against fate.

4. Characterization in the Present

The three-part structure of Pascual's story is also a function of the development of his character as narrator in the present. As Pascual recounts his past, at each stage he, or at least his account, emphasizes a different cause propelling him on his murderous course. As we have seen, in stage one he blames the position in society to which he is destined by birth; in stage two he blames Providence for the sheer bad luck that befalls him; and in stage three, as well as fate and society in general, in particular he blames other people for provoking him to violence. In the process he also develops a sporadic and increasing awareness of his own responsibility for what happened (*26*, p.658), the first sign of which is perhaps the Chispa episode. It is this growing feeling of guilt interspersed with the predominant feeling of grievance which appears to create conflict in Pascual's text and confusion in the reader's mind, a confusion which is compounded by uncertainty as to what Pascual's present situation is and what precisely is his intention as narrator. He does not make either very clear. What we do know is that he is in the condemned cell awaiting execution; we also know that he is given facilities to write (see the guard's letter) and that he is treated kindly by the prison chaplain who encourages him to go on writing (in Chapter 13). We can only presume that the external pressures exerted by such carrot-and-stick treatment are likely to produce equal uncertainty in Pascual's mind, but also at the same time provide the conditions for what is a remarkable development of his character as narrator of his own story.

This crucial aspect of Pascual's state of mind and situation as narrator has also thrown the critics into confusion. Whereas Beck thinks that despite his repentance Pascual naively puts himself in a good light when his actions show the opposite (*15*, p.285), Breiner-Sanders thinks he is naive in blaming himself and fate when society is responsible (*18*, p.133). Sobejano thinks Pascual's confession is naive because of its honesty, and in its confused counterpoint of love/hate and aggression/contrition Sobejano glimpses a moral and cathartic function of self-knowledge (*66*, pp.53–58). González and Thomas note a similar swing between hatred and guilt (*30*, pp.29–31,42–44; *70*, p.172), whilst Spires emphasizes a fluctuating tone of irony and anguish (*69*, p.50). Livingstone infers from Pascual's contradictory desire for verbal revenge and spiritual rehabilitation that he is both good and evil, simultaneously lying and baring his soul (*41*, pp.101–03). Jerez-Farrán tries to cut through the contradiction by asserting that Pascual's confession is nothing but a lie to save his neck (*38*, p.59), which echoes Soldevila's reference to the 'astucias y tácticas narrativas de Pascual, que cree lograr el indulto' (*67*, p.111). At the other extreme Penuel, like Ilie (*35*, p.39), rejects as implausible the attribution of narrative articulacy to a character whose development he thinks remains arrested at a primitive level (*55*, p.376).

But it is precisely this acquisition of narrative capability, not as a mere ploy, but as a means of self-knowledge and spiritual liberation that has been highlighted by Dougherty, who argues convincingly that Pascual becomes through his narration a very different person, morally, psychologically and intellectually, to his past self: 'al escribir sus memorias, Pascual renace y experimenta en su presente carcelario una libertad que desea perpetuar. Será este nuevo ser libre, no el criminal dominado por sus pasiones, a quien se ejecuta al final' (*24*, p.5). With strong support from others (e.g. *71*, pp.97, 114, 125; *34*, pp.10–11), Dougherty rightly stresses the intensity of Pascual's experience in prison because it produces a crisis of self-analysis and an increased consciousness of himself as a writer, especially in the most crucial chapter of all, Chapter 13, where Dougherty correctly sees, unlike Masoliver (*48*, p.7), an important tension arising between the religious and the literary confession. What Dougherty omits, though, is the real narrative and historical context which can help elucidate the conflict in Pascual's mind between religious piety and existential protest (also noted by *68*, p.300).

We have already seen how the opening phrase of Pascual's narrative is contextless and therefore incomprehensible to the first-time reader, though not to the anonymous *señor*, or to readers in 1942 who would have been sensitive to a context signalled by the initial letter from Badajoz prison in 1937. The second-time reader will at least understand Pascual's 'no soy malo, aunque no me faltarían motivos para serlo' in the context of the violence that leads to matricide. For Thomas (*70*, p.171) it is the memory of the matricide that provides unity to the text. But as Sobejano rightly insists (*66*, pp.23, 42), it is the context arising from the murder of Don Jesús that is freshest in Pascual's mind and therefore exerts a profound, even distorting, influence on his narrative. To borrow Zamora Vicente's memorable image, the figure of Don Jesús flits in and out the novel like a 'sombra encendida' (*74*, p.43). To argue, like some critics have done (*15*, p.288; *71*, p.117; *69*, pp.49–50; *18*, pp.123–25), that the last murder is not an essential part of the text is to ignore, amongst other things, the transcriber's pointed reference to the 'asesinato' and to the fact that Pascual fails to give any information about what motivated or provoked this last murder, 'los motivos que tuvo y los impulsos que le acometieron' (p.159). As in the case of Chispa where the 'motivos' were equally lacking, we can either skate over the problem of explaining the murder or try to fathom it out. But even if we accept the solution that Pascual's story is intended to enlighten the reader about the motives and impulses that led to the last crime, we are still faced with the difficulty of not knowing the purpose of Pascual's account. Is it self-justification or a confession of guilt? Like the dislocation at the end of Chapter 1, is the failure to narrate the last crime a symptom of lack of narrative control, or is it a calculated strategy? Is it an expression of Pascual's confusions, or a way of turning them to good effect?

To answer any of these questions we have to take a closer look at the sections of the text which give us a direct insight into Pascual's state of mind as narrator in the present, such as the prison interlude of Chapter 6. This reads on the surface like a straightforward prisoner's lament for lost freedom (*66*, pp.52–53). The problem here as elsewhere, however, comes from the preponderance of thoughts and feelings over factual information. Pascual expresses remorse, 'arrepentimiento' (p.60) and tries to elicit sympathy for his sorry state, his 'Mucha desgracia' (p.59); but the situation is not clarified, apart from the tantalizing references to being interrupted by 'interrogatorios y visitas del defensor' (p.59) and being transferred to a new and better place, 'el traslado a este nuevo sitio' (p.59), 'El sitio [...] es mejor' (p.60). The cause and significance of the move are unclear, though it could indicate some form of special treatment and encouragement given to Pascual by the authorities. Osuna's striking suggestion (*53*, p.87) that this marks the point when Pascual is first taken to Badajoz prison from wherever he was being held before (Torremejía perhaps), rather than explaining away, gives added external emphasis to the astonishing fact that Pascual has been moved to a better cell, to a room indeed with a view, and instead of being given short shrift is being encouraged to write at some length. From the reference to visits from a defending counsel, Urrutia, as we know (*71*, pp.57–60), infers that the initial purpose of Pascual's manuscript is an appeal against the death sentence. But even as we accept this helpful hypothesis, we can see that the precise form of the defence is no clearer in Chapter 6 than it was in Chapter 1, since Pascual now seems at this point to emphasize his repentant and lachrymose state rather more than his sense of injustice. A full knowledge of the context might help us define the precise effect that Pascual's prison lament has on us: is it poignant or cloying, is it genuine or hypocritical? But Pascual does not make the context clear, perhaps because he assumes it is clear to his reader, who he is sure will understand him: 'usted sabrá comprender lo que le digo' (p.61). And that is precisely the problem: the fictional reader must know much more and much worse about Pascual than the real reader, 'porque demasiado malos han de ser los informes que de mí conozca' (p.60). But our guess as to what reports the fictional *usted* has received cannot certainly be as good as Pascual's. We are left wondering whether the reader, be he a judge or perhaps the head of a military tribunal in Badajoz in 1937, would even bother to have read what Pascual writes. It may even be that Pascual is just as uncertain as we are about what he is doing. Does he think he is being encouraged to explain and justify himself, or make a full confession? Irrespective of what he would like to do, does he know which approach will impress his intended reader more? Is Pascual writing of his own volition, or has he been asked, or ordered, to write? We simply do not know; we can only guess. But what is clear in Chapter 6 is the growing confusion in Pascual's mind: 'Ahora, después de releer este fajo, todavía no muy grande, de cuartillas, se mezclan en mi cabeza las ideas más diferentes [...]' (p.59). As Dougherty points out (*24*), Pascual is his own first reader; and he is disconcerted by his own story because writing and reading force him to reflect on the past, introducing a tension between what he was and what he is. The major lesson he seems to have learnt by Chapter 6 is that the effort of reflection involved in writing should have been applied to controlling his actions in the past; he would not now be in prison.

The other prison interlude, Chapter 13, is extremely important for the insight it affords into Pascual's present state of mind. When he decides to break off writing for a month, the interruption of the story is much longer than in Chapter 6 and more pronounced, since the switch to the present time in Chapter 13 is preceded at the end of Chapter 12 by the extraordinary passage of hate beginning 'Se mata sin pensar' (p.102), where the narrative, having ground already to a halt, then changes abruptly from past tenses about specific people to an impersonal and abstract present. The breakdown of the narrative dramatizes stylistically what must be a corresponding breakdown in the narrator's mind: it is a point of crisis for both the narrative and the narrator.

Chapter 13 begins with Pascual informing us that during the month's inactivity he has found, or been invaded by, religious peace. He then asks for the chaplain to give him confession, and afterwards decides to take up the pen again. Apart from our ignorance as to what stage Pascual's judicial appeal might have reached and whether his latest state of mind is independent or not of legal events, what makes the chapter so puzzling is the confused state of mind it reveals. Pascual claims to have found religious tranquillity, but he then describes himself in a state of emotional and mental turmoil: 'Temblaba como si tuviera fiebre cuando un estado del alma se marchaba porque viniese el otro' (p.105). And the turmoil is paradoxically worse after taking confession, for he spends a sleepless night and is left in a deep depression, from which the only cure, he says, is to continue writing: 'como del aplanamiento en que me hundo no de otra manera me es posible salir si no es emborronando papel y más papel' (p.107). This is a decisive and enigmatic moment, for the resumption of the story depends on why the confession leaves Pascual in such a state. When he is given absolution, he says he feels embarrassed and ashamed — 'Pasé mucha vergüenza' (p.107) — and tries to repress in his mind certain 'pensamientos siniestros'; but what these thoughts are and why they occur to him he does not tell us. Beck seems right to suggest that the 'vergüenza' is caused by a resurgence of hatred which undermines the sincerity of the confession (*15*, p.288). But hatred of whom? We shall return to this shortly.

In order to have any chance of understanding what is going on here, we have to try and clarify the context by the same procedure we used to make sense of Chapter 1: that is, a reconstruction of chronology and psychology. Most of the critics who have studied this section of the novel would agree with Thomas's analysis (*70*, p.172) and see here, between Chapters 12 and 13, the coming to a head of Pascual's inner emotional conflict, with hate prominent at the end of 12 and guilt taking over in 13. But the limitation of Thomas's approach is his certainty that the only object here of Pascual's emotions is his mother, as well as a confusion over the significance of the transcriber's reference to purple ink, which leads Thomas to suspect that Chapters 12 and 13 may have been written at the end (*70*, p.175). Another critic, Schaefer, seems to assume the opposite: that these two chapters, with the confession of guilt, occur at the beginning (*64*, p.266–70). But since Chapters 12 and 13 are firmly situated in the narrative order as it stands, it makes much more sense to follow Dougherty (*24*) and interpret the purple ink as a way of highlighting not only Chapters 12 and 13 but also the chronological convergence with them of the covering letter. The main point then at issue is the precise point at which the covering

letter is to be relocated, for it matters a great deal whether we think
the letter was written immediately after the end of Chapter 12 (as a
conclusion), or after the month's break at the same time as Chapter
13 (as a new introduction).

Urrutia argues that the letter was written at the end of Chapter
12, when Pascual stops writing altogether, and that later he starts
again with the new purpose of explaining things to himself and
others (*71*, pp.60–62). The main difficulty here is the use of the
letter as evidence both for the definitive cessation of writing and its
resumption. By placing the letter between Chapters 12 and 13,
Urrutia weakens the force of the calculated effect the transcriber
says the letter is supposed to have. For, as I shall argue, the real
effectiveness of the letter comes from the way it anticipates the
problem of how the resumed text, and its conclusion, should be
read. Urrutia further weakens the significance of the letter and its
addressee by saying that the recipient of Pascual's resumed
narrative is now arbitrary. But his argument fails to undermine
Sobejano's view (*66*, pp.23–24) that the person still, or increasingly,
foremost in Pascual's mind has to be his last victim, Don Jesús,
whose name is so prominent in the letter. Pascual may no longer be
wanting a reprieve, or asking for forgiveness while alive — 'ya ni
pido perdón en esta vida' (p.17) — but he concludes the letter, on
the very same page, by sending his manuscript to Barrera López as
a plea for forgiveness to Don Jesús: 'y acoja este ruego de perdón
que le envía, como si fuera al mismo don Jesús, su humilde
servidor.'[13] The emphasis here on Pascual's relationship with his
last victim makes much more sense as a prologue to whatever is to
follow Chapter 13 rather than as an epilogue to what has preceded
it. And a further clue to the precise location of the letter can be
found in the prison guard's opinion that Pascual acted like a
madman but only after his first confession in prison: 'en cuanto que
lo hizo la primera se conoce que le entraron escrúpulos y

---

[13]I have corrected the Destino edition's 'como si fuera el mismo don
Jesús', since 'al' appears in the first and the author's definitive edition (*2*,
p.53), 'it' rather than *Vd* being understood as the subject of 'fuera'.
Uncorrected, the subject could also be Pascual (*48*, p.9).

remordimientos y quiso purgarlos con la penitencia' (p.163). When this is put alongside what Pascual says in his letter — 'quiero descargar, en lo que pueda, mi conciencia, con esta pública confesión, que no es poca penitencia' (p.15) — we can presume that the letter was written at the very same time as Chapter 13 and that both introduce us to a new and more self-conscious stage of Pascual's narrative, in which he is not simply addressing anybody (Urrutia's 'cualquiera') but making a public confession through Barrera López to everybody and especially Don Jesús. Whoever the *usted* is (the authority still in charge of the case or the general reader) he becomes a vehicle onto which Pascual projects or transfers his mental relationship with Don Jesús.

The essential clues to that relationship are to be found, I believe, in the letter and the dedication. At the start of the letter that ends with the plea for forgiveness there is a curious parenthesis after Don Jesús's name, '(que Dios haya perdonado, como a buen seguro él me perdonó a mí)' (p.15), which suggests that he has already received that forgiveness. Whilst this evident discrepancy creates a problem, it also provides a solution to the enigma of Don Jesús's smile in the dedication; for the smile is the one piece of evidence that supports Pascual's assertion that Don Jesús forgave him. So some are right to think that the dedication records a gesture of forgiveness from Don Jesús to his killer (*74*, pp.40–41; *53*, p.91; *57*, pp.74–75). But why then does Pascual request a forgiveness that has already been given? The answer must be that the Count's super-human gesture so haunts Pascual's mind that it continues to provoke guilt and a redoubled need to justify his action and have it forgiven.[14] Assuming that the letter and the dedication are indicative of the real narrative context, if we turn again to the main point of difficulty in Chapter 13, it is then extremely tempting to see some significance hidden in the immediate context of Pascual's

---

[14]The ambiguous syntax of the dedication might even conceal a pun on writing itself, with 'lo' referring to 'escrito', 'rematar' to finishing the text or/and killing again (*re*/*matar*) in the re-telling, with the memory of the smile having a direct effect on the ending. *P.D.* could also mean *postdata* (PS). Compare Lottini (*42*, p.58).

shame and sinister thoughts, that is, in the chaplain's words, 'Prepárate a recibir el perdón, hijo mío, [...] Reza conmigo el Señor mío, Jesucristo...' (p.107). My suggestion is that the emotions and thoughts that disturb Pascual's religious peace are linked, by association, to Christ's namesake, Don Jesús. Is Pascual's shame and guilt over the memory of his last victim so intense that the religious act of forgiveness is not enough? If so, does writing become then a form of extra repentance, as stated in the letter — 'no es poca penitencia' (p.15)? Or do the 'pensamientos siniestros' indicate something more sinister alongside the guilt? Renewed hatred, as Beck suggests? Or mixed emotions of hatred and guilt? (*34*, pp.5–6; *18*, p.137). It is obviously difficult to speculate about Pascual's feelings, but whatever they are, the object of his feelings has to be speculated upon as well.

And the same applies to the end of Chapter 12. Several critics (*17*, p.76; *46*, pp.44–46; *71*, p.61; *70*, p.172; *69*, pp.45–46) think that the temporary interruption here of the story is due entirely to the fact that it foreshadows the matricide, both in the past as a failed attempt, and in the present as an aborted sketch. There is much to be said for this view. Because the strange shift in the tenses and persons wrench the passage of hate out of its past context and place it not simply in a more vivid historic present, but in the narrator's real present, it can thus refer simultaneously to the murderous hatred felt in the past, from which Pascual runs away, and the actual matricide, which he is not yet ready to narrate directly. And certainly the transformation of the mother into an 'enemigo' is already prepared for in Pascual's analysis of his hatred in Chapter 5. However, the deliberate impersonality of the passage at the end of Chapter 12, serving to generalize personal experience (*22*, p.35), the use of exclusively masculine genders to describe the object of hate — 'el que va a ser el muerto', 'El enemigo' (p.102) — and Pascual's ulterior motives for writing what he writes in the condemned cell, all suggest to me that the text breaks down, not only through the collision of past with present and hatred with guilt, but also through a massive conflict and confusion in Pascual's head between the matricide and the murder of Don Jesús. But whatever is the primary object of Pascual's hatred, it is still remarkably difficult to sort out the meaning of every phrase in this convoluted passage. So convoluted, in fact, that the need to flee expressed at the end, whilst clarified obviously by Pascual's departure in Chapter 14, is also left dangling by the syntax in some future limbo, since it remains unclear whether the need to flee arises before or after the premeditated deed is done, or not done. For either is made possible by the tangle of negatives in the two contradictory paragraphs beginning with 'Pero'. If the passage does anticipate the matricide, as well as the last murder, I should also add that it does so in a way that anticipates the stylistic convolutedness and pointed ambiguity with which part of the matricide is narrated, as we shall see in a later chapter.

Despite differences of interpretation, there is common agreement that an important narrative crisis occurs in the gap between Chapters 12 and 13. Hatred has come into conflict with guilt, leading to confession, which in turn stimulates a fresh, even frenzied, desire to complete the rest of the story. What is not certain is whether the guilt is already so intense as to require further expiation in the form of a public confession, or whether it is intensified by renewed hatred. Even in the covering letter where the purpose of a confession is most manifest, there is a strong hint of persistent violent tendencies in Pascual's decision to accept the fate of execution, since 'es más que probable que si no lo hicieran volviera a las andadas'(p.17). Such thoughts may be similar to the 'pensamientos siniestros' mentioned in Chapter 13. If they are, the depression Pascual experiences immediately after confessing must be, as suggested, the result of a continuing conflict between guilty remorse and justified hatred, and it is this psychological tension that only further writing will help to alleviate.

Although Pascual's feelings are still confused, what is most important about Chapter 13 is the new confidence and awareness that he clearly feels about the story he is now resuming and his role as author. Several critics have remarked on the liberating, therapeutic and creative effects writing has for Pascual (*66*, p.58; *68*, p.294; *24*; *19*, p.97; *48*, p.7; *22*, pp.39–40; *40*, p.116; *60*, p.68).

But equally significant is how Pascual expresses it, for it is here that he makes a crucial comparison between the act of writing and the act of fathering a child. He says he wants to give proper care and attention to his manuscript because if he simply poured the story out onto paper, 'tan desmañado y deslavazado habría de quedar que ni su mismo padre — que soy yo — por hijo lo tendría' (pp.107–08). This is a point that has gone unnoticed and needs to be stressed: authorship begins to offer for Pascual a means of compensating for the failures of his past. It gives him a constructive, non-violent, way of satisfying his frustrated desire for paternity. His story has now become his pride and joy; he sees it, almost literally, as his brain-child, something he can leave behind for posterity.

The child analogy underlines what I have referred to as the fourth level, and fourth stage, of self-awareness in the development of Pascual's personality. Above all, it heralds a new awareness of the purpose of his narrative and his activity as narrator, both of which are redefined in the remaining paragraphs of Chapter 13. The first thing he notices is that the four months effort of writing (unlike anything else he has ever done before) has given him a new insight into the events of his past: 'cuando empezamos a trabajar sobre ellas [things in the past], nos presentan tan raros y hasta desconocidos aspectos, que de la primera idea no nos dejan a veces ni el recuerdo' (p.108). Sceptics might regard this as self-deception or hypocrisy on Pascual's part, as he appears to forget the gravity and horror of his crimes in order to concentrate on writing. But Pascual is far from forgetting his moral responsibility. On the contrary, he is aware that the emotional and mental distance created by writing enables him to transform the painful memory of the past into something useful, into the esthetic pleasure of art:

> No creo que sea pecado contar barbaridades de las que uno está arrepentido. Don Santiago me dijo que lo hiciese si me traía consuelo [...] Hay ocasiones en las que me duele contar punto por punto los detalles, grandes o pequeños, de mi triste vivir, pero, y como para compensar, momentos hay también en que con ello gozo

> con el más honesto de los gozares, quizá por eso de que
> al contarlo tan alejado me encuentre de todo lo pasado
> como si lo contase de oídas y de algún desconocido.
> (p.108–09)

Despite references to sin, repentance and the chaplain's encouragement, the function of writing here goes beyond a straightforward
confession; it is therapeutic (bringing 'consuelo'), because literary
detachment changes pain into pleasure ('el más honesto de los
gozares'), rather like the cathartic effect of tragedy whereby the
emotional reactions of pity and fear generate intellectual insight into
the significance of suffering. Though Beck sees too much irony to
find him tragic (*15*, p.287), several others have followed Marañón
(*45*) in emphasizing the tragic aspects of Pascual's character (*8*; *71*,
p.114; *41*, p.98). Pascual himself can be sensitive to irony, and goes
on here to answer a possible accusation of learning his lesson too
late ('en su boca se me imagina oír un a la vejez viruelas') by
insisting on the value of facing up to what has happened, on
confronting his past and present situation:

> pero hay que conformarse con lo inevitable, con lo que
> no tiene arreglo posible; a lo hecho pecho, y tratar de
> evitar que continúe, que bien lo evito aunque ayudado
> — es cierto — por el encierro (p.109).

Despite again the characteristic temporal ambiguity expressing
resignation to both a past and a present fate, and despite the
admission that imprisonment gives him no alternative, there is in
the phrase 'tratar de evitar que continúe' a positive aim of understanding past behaviour in order to show how it could have been
avoided, and, for others, still can be, for, as he has just suggested,
the story will help achieve insight into the atrocities ('barbaridades')
it narrates. Pascual here seems to realize what some critics do not: a
sense of tragedy involves not just inevitability, but also the reasons
for that inevitability. Much of course depends on how sympathetic
or sceptical we are towards the narrator, but it is at this point in

particular that we can glimpse, I suspect, just how much Pascual's intention and narrative pleasure might be shared by Cela (*19*, p.98).

What we see then in Chapter 13 is a considerable advance in the narrator's self-confidence as compared to the previous prison interlude of Chapter 6. There his mood was maudlin, his remorse full of nostalgia, and his mind thoroughly confused. Here in Chapter 13, out of crisis, confusion and depression there emerges a more positive and decisive tone, and, one feels, a crystallization of ideas. Instead of looking with nostalgia out of the cell window at what might have been, Pascual now looks ahead to finishing his story and, in the process, to working out his own conflicts and clarifying their significance for the reader. What I have called the fourth stage of Pascual's characterization may now perhaps be seen as two distinct phases. The initial growing awareness of his guilt and the accompanying confusion eventually generate, through the crisis of Chapter 13, a new phase of artistic self-awareness in which he is able to deal in a more detached and creative way with his own case in all its facets, no longer blaming his own nature, or nurture, or fate, or other people in isolation, but able to balance all of them together to form a complex self-portrait, of significance both for himself and the general reader.

It is curious nevertheless that just when Pascual as narrator displays much greater maturity, his outward behaviour, as we know, appears insane to the prison guard. This undoubtedly introduces a note of caution about Pascual's reliability as narrator. But is the guard himself a reliable judge? It seems ironic, after all, that Pascual's abnormality is most apparent when he ceases to act like a normal murderer. On the one hand the guard's amazement is justified by the fact that Pascual's behaviour is abnormal in the sense of exceptional, for as the guard says, 'fue el preso más célebre que tuvimos que guardar en mucho tiempo' (p.163). But on the other hand he is surely not justified in seeing Pascual's neurotic penances and compulsive writing as merely symptoms of mental illness; a more enlightened penologist would regard them as signs of moral health and psychological recovery, because Pascual is confronting himself and his crimes. Or is it, as the guard implies, more to do with a coward's fear of death and damnation? Perhaps it is both fear of death and a renewed zest for life, each producing the two kinds of behaviour witnessed by the guard: penitential self-abasement and literary self-assertion. From what the guard says we see the positiveness of Pascual's response to encouragement from the chaplain and prison director: 'El muy desgraciado se pasaba los días escribiendo, como poseído de la fiebre, y [...] se confiaba y no cejaba ni un instante' (p.164). It is quite clear that despite the insecurity of not knowing when his sentence will be carried out, an increasing atmosphere of security (in both senses of physical restraint and psychological support) instil enough confidence in Pascual for him to carry on writing with an enthusiasm that the guard mistakes for frenzy. The new urgency Pascual brings to his task can be seen also in his letter where, as we know, he addresses himself to the problem of where the story will end. At first sight the letter solves this problem in a very simple way. Pascual says he was initially worried by the fact that he could not narrate his own death, but decided to carry on regardless, leaving the ending to fate. But now he has taken the decision to stop writing, leaving what little remains to the reader's imagination. The impression given is one of a story completed as far as it is possible to complete, and of a voluntary choice of ending by the narrator. We know however that this effect was calculated when the letter was composed (at the same time as Chapter 13) in order, we can see now, to circumvent the probability of Pascual's own death bringing the story to an abrupt and involuntary end. The important questions, as I noted in the Introduction, are these: did the execution prevent Pascual from completing the story and is the ending therefore arbitrary; did he have time to write more pages which were then lost, as the transcriber asks twice (pp.158–59); or is the ending as Pascual intended it to be when he wrote the letter?

Elsewhere (*34*, p.7) I have attempted an answer by highlighting the following sentence in Pascual's letter :

me he metido a contar aquella parte que no quiso
borrárseme de la cabeza y que la mano no se resistió a

> trazar sobre el papel, porque otra parte hubo que al
> intentar contarla sentía tan grandes arcadas en el alma
> que preferí callármela y ahora olvidarla. (pp.15–16)

Pascual prefaces this with the admission that lapses of memory may
have led to his omitting some events from his story. But here he
goes on to state, firstly, that he has in fact narrated that part of his
life which was unforgettable, and secondly, that there was another
part which, though unforgettable, he has deliberately chosen to
suppress ('preferí callármela') because the attempt to relate it made
him feel like retching ('arcadas'). What might this sickening and
self-censored part be? Is it an omission that has occurred, logically,
before the letter was written? Urrutia (*71*, p.112) mistakenly thinks
so, identifying it as the full version of the matricide omitted at the
end of Chapter 12. Or is it something whose omission Pascual plans
ahead and whose effect he deliberately calculates in advance? The
only episode of Pascual's story that is significantly conspicuous by
its absence is of course the murder of Don Jesús. My belief that this
is the part Pascual chooses to suppress is encouraged by the
transcriber's remark that nothing is known about the motives
behind the last crime precisely because Pascual dug his heels in and
chose not to reveal them: 'Pascual se cerró a la banda y no dijo esta
boca es mía más que cuando le dio la gana, que fue muy pocas
veces' (p.159). These two quotations are also used by Osuna to
argue the same case, except that for him the suppression of the
murder has no real implications for Pascual's characterization; Cela
is simply censoring the political motivation for the killing (*53*,
p.90–91).

My own hypothesis, however, is that Pascual at the time he
composes the letter and resumes his story in Chapter 13 has decided
for his own autonomous reasons where his story will end, that is,
after the matricide and before the murder of Don Jesús. He decides
to omit the latter crime because for him it is too sickening. There is
of course an element of scandalous irony in the idea that anything
could be more nauseating than the matricide or the other crimes that
are narrated. Yet Pascual's reason can be seen to ring

psychologically true if we assume two things: that the last murder was indeed even more horrific and grisly than the others, and that Pascual is more sickened by it because it provokes in him a much greater feeling of guilt. There is still the possibility (though increasingly remote) that Pascual may be feigning nausea because he may be feigning guilt. But giving him the benefit of the doubt, let us speculate briefly on what might be the intended effect of his deliberate omission.

If, as we have seen in Chapter 13, Pascual is undergoing a genuine conflict between the need to confess his guilt and the need to justify his hatred, with regard not only to the past, but also, and especially, to his most recent victim, then the omission of this last murder could be a method of dealing with that conflict by having it both ways, atoning for the murder by refusing to relive it, and at the same time using the narrative of the matricide as an outlet for the feelings of justified hatred that presumably led to the murder of Don Jesús in the first place. This would provide Pascual with psychological therapy; it would also, at the same time, avert the threat of censorship against an attempted justification of a revolutionary killing, and would offer resistance to those in authority who might want him to confess to the killing as a psychotic and criminal act. Since we do not know for certain how Pascual might have narrated his last crime (justifying it in socio-political terms, or condemning it as an atrocity), and given that Cela, in either case, would probably have met with the barrier of censorship ('Barrera' López?), I would argue, as I started to do in my Introduction, that Cela makes a literary virtue out of necessity by giving Pascual convincing reasons for the omission, both psychological, because it is therapeutic, and literary, because it creates ambiguity and complexity.

Moreover, Pascual's character as narrator acquires further depth and consistency if we realize that his preoccupation with the ending is a psychological necessity as well. This can be seen in the letter when he says he has been driven mad by the idea that 'mis actos habían de ser, a la fuerza, trazados sobre surcos ya previstos' (p.16). Here he is not referring to any predestination of his past actions by fate, as some mistakenly think (*68*, p.293; *70*, p.167; *47*, p.98; *31*, p.3; *30*, pp.25–26), but to his present activity of writing, the duration of which he knows is determined by those who will decide his fate, that is, the date of his execution. Hence Pascual's determination in Chapter 13 to finish his task, to 'dar un empujón a estas memorias para ponerlas en el camino del fin' (p.107), lest his story be interrupted and left incomplete, 'a la mitad y como mutilada'. Pascual wants to preempt the ending before the executioner brings his life to an end. And this is one of the main reasons for Pascual's passionate and frantic involvement in his narrative: it gives him the opportunity to defend himself against those who control his fate by exerting his own authorial control, not just over his life-story as Buckley has perceptively stated (*19*, p.97), but also more specifically over the final outcome of the story, by deciding himself how it will end, and in a way that will assert his own freedom from authority. In the course of his story Pascual has shown how his life has been determined by the various factors we have noted: birth, upbringing, Providence, fate, the behaviour of others, and his own violent impulses. But now, as others exert total (and totalitarian) control over his physical self, the act of writing gives him the power to shape his own narrated destiny, responding in his own way to their carrot-and-stick coercion. Pascual, it seems to me, realizes that if he cannot save his neck he can at least do two things: escape the brainwashing of his jailers and cheat death through a posthumous survival in a work of literature. This artistic self-awareness and autonomy are the privileges that Cela bestows on his fictional creature.

I am arguing, therefore, that Pascual's ending is both psychologically crucial and artistically calculated, and its full significance depends, as Pascual hints in the letter, on the reader's collaboration. When Pascual says that there will be little left to reconstruct, he is anticipating the future gap at the end and is indicating that the story, though incomplete, can be completed by the reader through an imaginative reconstruction of what is there, and not there, in the text. This involves not only the reconstruction of the omitted crime but also its relationship to the ending as it stands, to the matricide, and that connection, as I have already argued, is first adumbrated in the shadowy outline of the body of the hated enemy in Chapter 12. Indeed this passage may even provide textual evidence for Pascual's aborted attempt — 'al intentar contarla' (p.15) — to narrate the last sickening murder. But the success of Pascual's remarkable strategy, and the validity of my hypothesis, depends very much on whether it is possible to perceive some trace of the suppressed memory of the last murder not just in Chapter 12 but more crucially in the full-blown account of the matricide. This will be discussed in the next chapter.

Before that a brief mention of another curious incident, and a minor form of prison interlude, in Chapter 17, which involves a further but less important problem for the narrator's manuscript. Here Pascual, rather self-righteously, criticizes the wickedness of whoever has stolen some pages of his manuscript. Apparently three chapters have disappeared: the one in which the passage occurs and the next two, that is, if the order is correct, Chapters 18 and 19. In re-writing these chapters Pascual tells us he has added certain 'filosofías' (p.133), referring specifically to the long second paragraph of Chapter 17, in which he reflects on the irony of the fact that the reduction of his prison sentence for the murder of Estirao, rather than doing him a favour, exposed him to the risk of committing more crimes, such as the matricide, and whatever crime has caused him not to be 'con la cabeza tan segura sobre mis hombros como al nacer' (p.132), that is, to be in danger of execution for the murder of Don Jesús. Pascual seems to suggest that the prison authorities were too lenient and should have kept him locked up for much longer. Virtually in the same breath he complains about society's lack of compassion for him, for 'este pobre yo, este desgraciado derrotado que tan poca compasión en usted y en la sociedad es capaz de provocar' (p.133). What has Pascual in mind? That the authorities should show compassion by reprieving him from the death sentence, but not fall into the previous error of giving him an early parole? And what else does he have in mind? The word 'derrotado' not only means a victim of society in general, but also resonates with the more immediate historical situation in 1937 (and 1942), in which the military victors faced the same dilemma of how to treat the defeated, with a rigorous repression or with a more enlightened compassion. Several more points emerge with regard to the 'filosofías' added in the re-writing of Chapter 17. Firstly, rather than being a clumsy attempt to lessen the incongruity of an illiterate yet sophisticated narrator (*68*, p.295), they support Dougherty's view (*24*) that this is another important section of the novel where Pascual comments on his own text, but they fail to support Dougherty's rider that the revision of the last three chapters adds nothing significantly new, for the 'filosofías' show Pascual reflecting, as we have just seen, on his immediate situation and the relevance to it of the wider issue of crime and punishment. Secondly, we see that Pascual has not abandoned entirely his earlier position of complaint in favour of the guilt and resignation to the death sentence proclaimed in Chapter 13 and the covering letter; he is still capable of feeling very sorry for himself and placing the blame on society, fate and others, specifically in this case on the anonymous *usted*, who appears to have the power of life or death over Pascual. In any case, whether the readership is alive or posthumous, Pascual takes the opportunity of reminding it about the complexity of causes behind his present plight. And two final points that bring me back to the problems involved in Pascual's manuscript. One is that Pascual's outcry against the theft, though it might be construed as outrageous moral hypocrisy on his part, further demonstrates the huge psychological investment he has made in a narrative which he is so determined to complete. The other is that the reader, whose attention has been drawn to these added reflections in Chapter 17, should also be alerted to the possibility that Pascual might have added similar, more general, and contemporary, reflections to the re-written versions of the last two chapters. This consideration, as we shall soon see, will be especially relevant to our reading of the final chapter; for re-writing must have given Pascual even more time to consider the relevance of his ending to the sickening 'otra parte' he has decided to suppress, and thereby add an even wider dimension of meaning to the ending than perhaps he originally conceived of back in Chapter 13.

5. Senses of an Ending (Chapter 19)

At the beginning of Chapter 19 we find Pascual is now married to Esperanza after their brief meeting in Chapter 18. But instead of describing the marriage, Pascual moves immediately into defining his feelings of hatred for his mother in several obscure passages of difficult prose over-clotted with abstractions. Then the narrative becomes much simpler and more specific as it accelarates into the final dramatic climax of the matricide. But once we have got over the shock of a first reading and look back to discover what in actual fact provokes the hatred and causes the murder, we find that although Pascual may have successfully conveyed his own state of mind, he has conspicuously failed, as Alborg says (*13*, pp.85–86), to give us a convincing explanation of the circumstances that led to the final deterioration of the relationship with his mother. The little objective information he does provide is restricted to virtually the first paragraph; we are simply told that two months after the wedding Pascual's mother has gone back to her old ways — 'seguía usando de las mismas mañas y de iguales malas artes que antes de que me tuvieran encerrado' (p.149). Her words constantly wound or irritate him, and the crunch seems to come when the tension between the mother and the new daughter-in-law becomes so unbearable that Esperanza serves Pascual with an ultimatum — 'me planteó la cuestión' (p.149) — presumably along the lines of 'either she goes or I go'. The other eminently sensible alternative Pascual thinks about is for the pair of them to move far away from his mother's house. Why they do not is a mystery; Pascual simply says, 'la cosa la fui aplazando, aplazando'. We know nothing more about the marital situation, or the mother's allegedly provocative behaviour, or the chronology involved.

What little detail there is might just be, however, the tip of an iceberg. For it is conceivable that behind the vague and sporadic

references to months, weeks and days passing, there might be a
gradual, incident-strewn development of tension over a significant
span of time. Could it be that the initial reference to two months of
marriage obscures the possibility that there was ample time after
that for the second marriage to be plagued by similar frustrations to
those that happened in the first, namely the failure to produce viable
offspring? From the information we get in Chapter 17 that Pascual
renewed his acquaintance with Don Conrado 'tres años y medio más
tarde' (p.137), we can infer that the marriage lasted at least three
years before matricide sent Pascual back to Chinchilla prison. But
the only vestiges of the possibility of further children are, firstly, the
glimpse of children playing in the square that makes Pascual pause
for thought on the fatal day, secondly, the suggestive image (in the
fourth paragraph) of 'ese osario de esperanzas muertas, al poco de
nacer, que — ¡desde hace tanto tiempo ya! — nuestra triste vida es'
(p.150), and, thirdly, and retrospectively, the intriguing use of a
plural in the description of the kitchen back in Chapter 1: 'y los
chiquillos, cuando los tuve, también tiraban para allí en cuanto se
despegaban de la madre' (p.25). This plural could well be an over-
sight (*50*, p.52) by either narrator or author, since in the rest of the
text only one child (Pascualillo) survives beyond birth. But the rest
of the passage seems particularly careful, especially in its refusal to
identify the mysterious 'alguien' who preferred not to sleep in the
bedroom vacated by Pascual's parents. Urrutia thinks Pascual may
well have had several children with Esperanza and omitted the fact
as irrelevant (*71*, p.112). There is of course precious little to go on
in the three details quoted; but at least this is one occasion when a
reconstruction of objective reality might work for and not against
Pascual by revealing mitigating circumstances. This is not futile
speculation, because we know by now that children and the ability
to father them are a central obsession with Pascual.[15] But even if he

---

[15]L.C. Knight's 1933 essay, 'How Many Children Had Lady Macbeth?',
Explorations (Harmondsworth: Penguin, 1964), pp.13–50, criticizes studies
of character which fail to treat a text as a unity. But unanswerable
questions about Pascual's character are raised as an integral part of this
novel by the convention of textual unity.

did have more children, he has signally failed to inform us about
them.

So instead of presenting us with a clear objective description
of events preceding the matricide, Pascual concentrates on his own
subjective state, and uses various rhetorical devices to force the
reader to experience the same emotions revolving round the one
basic idea that hatred can be so overwhelming as to make murder
inevitable. Faced with the obvious gap between subjective rhetoric
and objective reality, it is quite right for sceptical readers to suspect
one of two things: either Pascual is too confused to understand the
reality of the situation, as Beck argues (*15*, p.296), or that all of his
special pleading is quite consciously aimed at distracting attention
away from his lack of motivation and the inescapable conclusion
that the mother simply becomes a scapegoat for Pascual's own
problems, another victim of her son's psychotic character. Yates has
voiced this scepticism in the following appreciative way:

> Given as flat *données*, from a conventional third-person
> perspective, the themes of Pascual as a man predestined
> to murder his mother and of her death as something
> fatally preordained would surely be highly melodramatic
> and unconvincing. The logic of the first-person mode on
> the other hand makes all this credible in Cela's novel
> [...] it is perfectly consistent or 'realistic' for Pascual, in
> his confession, to present his *a posteriori* knowledge as
> an *a priori* fatal determinism which diminishes his own
> responsibility [...] *Pascual Duarte* simply will not go
> into the third person: we could paraphrase the story, but
> we should lose virtually all the suggestiveness which
> [...] is an integral function of Cela's technique. (*73*,
> pp.18–19)

This confirms that Pascual is successful at communicating his
subjectivity, whilst objectively he remains an unreliable and possibly
self-deceiving narrator. But this otherwise perceptive analysis
ignores what is the central problem with Pascual's narrative

technique in Chapter 19: not the subjectivity of the first-person mode (where it is used at the end we get a clear picture of what happens) but the degree of abstraction created by a rhetorical use of first-person plural and third-person modes along with present and future tenses, highly reminiscent of the difficult passage at the end of Chapter 12. Indeed, much of the chapter's suggestiveness comes from the rhetoric that deflects from the linear accuracy of the first-person narrative, exposing it to charges of distortion or confusion. And this deflection, it seems to me, is caused by hindsight not just after the event (the matricide), but also, more crucially, after, for Pascual, much more recent events, producing as a result, not so much the confused labyrinth of ideas criticized by Beck (*15*, p.296) as the intricate entanglement of recollection and anticipation emphasized by Livingstone (*41*, pp.98–99). Let us look closer at the main examples of stylistic and mental contortion.

The first one occurs with the heavily insistent use of the word *tierra*, particularly in the phrase 'poner la tierra por en medio'. It refers initially to the possibility of Pascual leaving home and putting distance between himself and domestic conflict. Then at the end of paragraph two, in an abrupt change of temporal perspective, *tierra* is used to express the impossibility of escape from the guilty conscience that presumably arises from the eventual outcome of that conflict: 'La tierra que no tuvo largura ni anchura suficiente para hacerse la muda ante el clamor de mi propia conciencia...' (pp.149–50). Then paragraph three switches to another impossibility, that of putting 'tierra' between (separating oneself from) one's own shadow or past self; impossible, that is, unless suicide is contemplated, which seems to be the case in the fourth paragraph: 'Hay ocasiones en las que más vale borrarse como un muerto, desaparecer de repente como tragado por la tierra' (p.150). By this point the rhetorical froth worked up by the use of *tierra* six times within the space of a page has obscured from view the circumstances and sequence of events that might help to explain, among other things, why there is a discrepancy between the guilty conscience referred to here and a later sentence that asserts just the opposite: 'Pero de aquellos actos a los que nos conduce el odio [...]

no tenemos que arrepentirnos jamás, jamás nos remuerde la conciencia' (p.153). Such a flagrant contradiction may be explained away as only a temporary conflict (*18*, pp.98–99), but two other explanations seem more likely: either it betrays Pascual's mental instability and deviousness; or, more probably, it comes from the effect of merging together two separate periods of time, before and after the same event.

Clearly one of the main causes of difficulty is this temporal imprecision, which Foster explains as the confusion of past and present occurring in the intensity of matricide (*27*, p.32). The imprecision increases in the third paragraph, at the phrase 'este mí mismo del que, de quitarle la sombra y el recuerdo, los nombres y los cueros, tan poco quedaría' (p.150), with its sudden switch to a present conditional whose relationship to the past remains uncertain. Does the idea of suicide raised here in the third, and continued with exclusively present tenses in the fourth paragraph, refer to a time before the matricide, or after it, when guilt has taken over? If after, as seems to be the case, where is the temporal present of the whole of the fifth paragraph to be located? For the idea of suicide, which has been carried over into it, gradually changes into the idea of murder. Has time shifted back to before the event, as now seems the case? Does the mood of suicidal, guilt-induced, depression lead on to hatred and matricide, or does it occur after?

The extraordinarily complicated fourth and fifth paragraphs are not only disorientating from a temporal and conceptual perspective, they are also syntactically disconcerting through their insistent and imprecise use of abstract nouns and unspecified pronouns. This type of syntax intensifies the narrative shift into an internalized, highly abstracted, present; and as a result both paragraphs develop into what are virtually self-contained prose poems. The fourth paragraph, for instance, is full of a baroque pessimism, with heavy references to sin, the corruption of the flesh, and the stench of a guilty conscience. Especially noticeable is the way in which the stench of guilt not only emanates from Pascual's past actions, but is also thrust by the syntax right under the reader's nose. Indeed, the impersonal and first-person plural forms might

appear to include the reader as one of the sources of the smell. Of
course, the power of the rhetoric to involve and implicate the reader
depends on how much readers are, or were, willing to identify themselves with the kind of experience Pascual is trying, through his
narrative style, to generalize. Ilie simply dismisses this passage for
being too much out of Pascual's rustic character, whilst remarking
on the ontological subtlety of the previous third paragraph (*35*,
pp.44, 75) (cf. *18*, pp.60–63, 127).

The fifth paragraph, beginning 'La idea de la muerte' (p.150),
is the longest, the most convoluted and the most abstract of all, and
the one in which the use of first-person plural verbs is most
insistent. As a result, it is not clear who is feeling and thinking what
towards whom. The whole paragraph is given a systematically
shifting meaning by the ambiguity of the concepts used and the
imprecision of the context. Even though the context will be
specified in the next paragraph as Pascual's hatred for his mother
before the matricide, in this paragraph the first concept of 'La idea
de la muerte', modulating into 'las ideas que nos trastornan' and
'Los pensamientos que nos enloquecen', all seem to mean an
awareness of one's own mortality, referring back to the previous
context of suicidal depression that occurs we do not know whether
after or before the matricide. However, these ideas are soon clarified
as being responsible for someone else's death, 'la ideas que han de
ocasionar el que nos corten la cabeza donde se cocieron'. Then one
day things get much worse, 'el mal crece', 'mal' in any or all senses
of the word: damage, disease or evil. Shortly after, it develops into
'el odio que nos mata'. Is this someone else's hate, or our hate, that
is killing us? Does it kill us literally or figuratively speaking? The
object of hate is then defined as 'El enemigo'. Although pangs of
conscience have been mentioned ('nos duele la conciencia'), the
prospect of disaster is viewed with a sado-masochistic pleasure: 'La
desgracia es alegre, acogedora, y el más tierno sentir gozamos en
hacerlo ['lo' referring to 'el sentir'?] arrastrar sobre la plaza
inmensa de vidrios que va siendo ya nuestra alma.' The paragraph
ends with the beginning of a lethal fall, headlong into hell, 'el
infierno' presumably in a literal posthumous sense, though a

figurative one (hell on earth) cannot be excluded. The difficulties of making sense of this crucial fifth paragraph are obvious. The lack of a clear temporal and conceptual link with the subsequent context of Pascual's wish to kill his mother could be put down simply to bad writing. On the other hand, one might see the devices that wrench the passage out of the narrative context as admirable ways of making the past vividly present to the reader, a form of historic present. But neither alternative would fully explain the deliberate ambiguity of the writing, or the mistaken assumption that matricide will lead to execution ('el que nos corten la cabeza'), because Pascual, we remember, has already done thirteen years in prison for that crime.

There must be more to these passages than just a slipshod account of his feelings before and after the matricide. My own repeated reaction, on re-reading this chapter, is to admire the power of the writing to generalize the particular, giving Pascual's hatred and guilt the resonance of myth. By concentrating attention overwhelmingly on the experience taking place in the narrator's heart and mind, attached to, but abstracted from, the concrete and abnormal circumstances of matricide, the narrative invites the reader to identify imaginatively with part at least of the same experience (*18*, pp.117–18). Though none of us (I assume) are murderers, most of us will feel occasionally like murdering someone, and apart from moral scruples, which almost prevent Pascual from doing the deed (*22*, pp.36–37), one of the reasons we do not carry rage into action is our anticipation of the experience he attains only by hindsight. The act of writing and re-writing (as implied by Chapter 17) enables him, as Dougherty says (*24*), to explore various explanations for the matricide: sin, pleasure, fate, and circumstance. But in the light of the sentence, 'volverme atrás […] me hubiera conducido a la muerte, quién sabe si al suicidio' (p.153), Pascual also comes to realize that, having reached a situation in which the only alternative seemed to be to kill or commit suicide, the choice of murder was not only inevitable, it turned out to be just another form of suicide, a kind of living hell, leading inexorably to self-hate and self-destruction — 'el odio que nos mata' (p.151). What seemed the only solution at the time was really the worst solution, or no solution at all. The insight Pascual is groping towards is not that there was no other choice, as some critics see it (*18*, pp.107–08; *70*, pp.173–74), but that his own psychological state, which he dwells on so intensely, prevented him from seeking and seeing an alternative way out of the impasse. Looking back he can certainly remember what it felt like to be in an impossible situation and to seek relief by eliminating his mother altogether. But hindsight tells him there was no lasting relief, that what he did was not only wicked but essentially stupid; for which ultimately he has only himself to blame. This difficult admission is reached even at the same time as he remembers vividly the feeling of having no other alternative, in what Livingstone rightly calls an 'inextricable mixture of fatality and wilfulness' (*41*, p.99). The most relevant passage is the seventh paragraph, when 'la idea de la muerte de mi madre' is described as 'algo fatal que había de venir y que venía, que yo había de causar y que no podía evitar aunque quisiera, porque me parecía imposible cambiar de opinión, volverme atrás, evitar lo que ahora daría una mano porque no hubiera ocurrido' (p.152). In now regretting what happened, Pascual can see quite clearly, more clearly than many critics would give him credit for (*15*, p.297), that his own judgement ('opinion'), premeditation and sado-masochistic enjoyment ('gozaba en provocar con el mismo cálculo y la misma meditación'), were decisive factors in what was felt to be, much more at the time than after, an unstoppable sequence of events leading towards murder. Moreover, the precisely defined paradox of free will and fate is not only remarkably honest, its relevance goes beyond this individual case: it can apply equally well to similar acts of violence which seem inevitable through the blinkered perceptions and perverse self-indulgence of those who commit them.

Pascual's awareness of his own responsiblity and its wider application can be seen in the *tierra* image already discussed. As well as denoting his 'culpa' (p.149), one also notes the strong cultural, almost mythical, resonance of its use in the context of hatred for the mother. For there is an echo here of both Machado's

'La tierra de Alvargonzález' (the legendary parricide in the
accursed lands of Castile) (*53*, p.96) and the question asked by the
Cain-like hero at the end of Unamuno's *Abel Sánchez*: '¿Qué leche
mamé? [...] '¿Por qué nací en tierra de odios?'[16] One is tempted
then to see a similar sort of racial and geographical determinism:
Pascual's life is shaped by his hateful mother, and, at a symbolic
level, by the violent curse of his Spanish motherland. But it is only
an echo. Pascual now prefers to emphasize a different tradition,
using suitably baroque word-play on the image of *tierra* to define
very precisely the extent of his own responsibility. The phrase
'poner la tierra por en medio' denotes his two alternatives, distance
or death, and the fact that he chooses the latter course, of his own
volition, no matter how influenced by the inherent nature of his
mother/land, is explicitly conveyed by the inability of the *tierra* to
absorb the sound of his guilty conscience afterwards, as seen in the
phrase already quoted (pp.149–50). Perhaps it is Pascual's insight
into his own guilt that enables him in the final page to catch a more
charitable glimpse of his odious mother, when Esperanza's lamp
lights up the mother's purple face, 'morada como un hábito de
nazareno' (p.156), and the taste of the blood spurting from her
throat is likened to the blood of slaughtered lambs, 'sabía lo mismo
que la sangre de los corderos' (p.157). We shall return to the
Christian symbolism in the Conclusion.

One can of course read other dimensions of meaning into the
act of matricide. For some it represents Pascual's existential self-
affirmation and liberation from the past (*51*, p.220; *69*, pp.48–49).
Some may see the same sexual symbolism as Bernstein (*17*,
pp.80–81; *16*, pp.306–08; *55*, p.370) and the parallel he draws with
the myth of Orestes (who killed his mother to avenge his father's
murder). Others may prefer a Freudian application of the myth of
Oedipus (who unwittingly killed his father and married his mother).
In using the term 'Oedipus complex' to define Pascual's hatred of
his mother (*8*; *49*) we must not forget that Freud's theory stresses
the triangular nature of the child's relationship with *both* parents,

[16]Miguel de Unamuno, *Obras completas* (Madrid: Esceliecer, 1966), II,
p.758.

and that the role of the father may be taken by a father-figure, that
is, Don Jesús (*34*). Jerez Farrán tries out a different complex, that of
the devouring (castrating?) mother (*38*, pp.54–55), but still sees that
there must be a parallel between Pascual's conflict with his mother
and his rebellion against the parental authority of Don Jesús (*38*,
p.57). But to what extent might such a parallel be supported by the
text? As an explanation of the process leading to matricide, the
narrative seems hopelessly confused; but if the experience of that
process is reduplicated elsewhere (in the future and in others), then
the confusions may be regarded as artistically deliberate and therefore more meaningful. Although the rest of the chapter reinserts the
narrative back into the concrete situation of the matricide in the
past, the intervening paragraphs of abstraction have held up the
action and done damage to the linear realism of the text to such an
extent that we are encouraged to wonder whether the whole of this
episode is being narrated, at least sporadically, on three simultane-
ous levels: literal, metaphorical, and mythical.

The guilty insight Pascual displays in this chapter is acquired,
as I have said, after the event, possibly a long time after the event.
The suspicion arises that through and beyond the process of
abstraction to which the literal reality is subjected, there is indeed a
figurative link with something else. That is, the ideas of death and
murderous hatred are directed at more than one 'enemigo' (p.151),
at two enemies, one in the past (the mother), the other in the present
(Don Jesús), with the literal reality of the first functioning also as a
metaphor for the second. And another part of the figurative
dimension may relate not solely to the object of hatred but also to
the subject who feels it. We have seen how the syntactical involvement of the reader in Pascual's experience is not just for the sake of
vividness since it suggests that his hatred of the enemy can be
shared on a more general or mythical level. But there is also a more
immediate historical relevance: for the contemporary reader in 1942
there was not only a World War raging, there was the traumatic
memory of the recent civil war, at the begining of which, as we
should constantly remind ourselves, is located the crime that will
ensure Pascual's execution and, so he fears, his eternal damnation

to hell.

Awareness of this context should also make us sensitive to anything that might be construed as figurative in the rest of an otherwise straightforward narrative, tied down chronologically to the precise date of 'el 10 de febrero de 1922' (p.153). Besides the example of 'enemigo', there is Pascual's decision to use a knife, 'hacer uso del hierro', as the only way to stop the rot, 'al mal había que sangrarlo' (p.152), which recalls the political cliché of resorting to the iron surgery of military intervention. And when Pascual, after hovering on the brink for what seems an age, is precipitated by the sound of the floor creaking into what he describes as 'la lucha más tremenda que usted se puede imaginar' (p.156), we are bound to wonder whether it really would have been so difficult for the fictional *usted* in 1937 and the reader in 1942 to imagine anything as tremendous (*tremendista*?). More symbolism can be seen at the end when Pascual extinguishes the lamp held by Esperanza, his last glimmer of hope. This example is embarrassingly obvious, but it encourages a symbolic reading of what has gone before.

At a figurative level, then, there are suggestive echoes of the wider historical situation of passionate hatred that led to the inferno of civil war. There are no doubts in Champeau's mind that this is so: 'el matricidio simboliza la guerra civil, una vida dominada por *el odio*' (22, p.32). Indeed, the psychological process underlying the matricide can be seen as analogous to a collective psychopathology of violent conflict. The three levels through which Pascual's behaviour passes — the idea of hatred, degenerating into a question of 'amor propio', of willing himself to overcome moral scruples, and then naked eroticized aggression — might be compared to the general phenomenon of hatred arising from ideas (i.e. an ideological polarization) generating an uncompromising struggle of wills, and finally a sadistic orgy of killing (see *12*, p.280). One difficulty in linking Pascual's psychology to the collective is his suicidal despair, which is easier to envisage after the euphoria of war than before; but it may apply in the sense that violence can be fuelled by feelings of despair, and by a collective willingness to commit political suicide.

The crucial mediating link, of course, between the individual and the collective is the hidden presence in Pascual's mind of the last crime. But in many ways it is easier to imagine the generalization of his matricidal hate to the wider conflict than it is to see the precise fit of an analogy, if one exists, between the matricide and the murder of Don Jesús. It depends on our readiness to see the structure of Pascual's narrative ending as a form of metaphor; for it is the omission of the last murder that stimulates us to complete what appears incomplete by looking for signs that some properties of the suppressed event have been transferred to, or substituted by, the events that are narrated. I have already speculated in the previous chapter that this is precisely the strategy for finishing his story that occurs to Pascual when he resumes writing in Chapter 13. He expresses remorse by cutting out the last crime, and at the same time expresses the hatred that led to it by transferring it onto the matricide. This seems to me to provide the only hypothesis capable of making complete sense of Pascual's role as narrator. But the main difficulty here, as is often the case with metaphor, is that the nature of the two terms identified are so discordant that their connection seems too far-fetched to be credible. Not only is there a gap in the text where the last crime should have been narrated, there is an enormous semantic gap between on the one hand the psychopathic murder of a mother (an odious peasant woman) and on the other the revolutionary killing of a local figurehead (a rich and respectable nobleman). The matricide cannot be read simply as a straightforward metaphor for the struggle of a revolutionary peasantry against the ruling class, however appealing such an interpretation might be, since the flimsiness of specific motivation for the matricide will tend to cast a correspondingly negative light on revolutionary activity. The strategy adopted by Sobejano and Champeau is to avoid the pitfalls of analogy by setting up the last two crimes as parallel, but separate, symbols: Don Jesús represents the attack on the ruling class, and the mother the backward society that has to be destroyed (*66*, p.31; *22*, p.41). But Champeau, in attempting to rationalize Pascual's obsessive hatred through generalization (*22*, p.32), shows how difficult it is to keep the matricide separate from the civil war killing of Don Jesús.

If we try to sort out a significant connection between the last two crimes, we have to confront the paradoxical fact that the matricide, the crime that is narrated, may seem even less understandable than the murder that is omitted. To extrapolate from Pascual's previous behaviour explanations for the matricide (as I did in Chapter 3) is perhaps even more problematic than to speculate about the historically more understandable context of civil war for the last crime. The pathological hatred Pascual shows towards his mother, by obscuring from view the psychological consistency of his action (based on his paternity complex), acts as a cautionary counterweight to the imaginatively more appealing, because politically motivated, killing. To put it bluntly: the representative normality of the murder of don Jesús (normal in the context of civil war) is undermined and contradicted by the abnormality of the matricide. As Yates suggests (73), there is a disturbing shift from the previous crime to the later one, and then back again.[17]

So the potentially metaphorical structure of the ending poses a problem of logic by proposing an identity between two things that are disconcertingly different. The extent to which we can see a link between the psychotic matricide and the political parricide depends on how pointed is the omission of one of them, and on how loaded with ulterior meaning are the passages that ostensibly refer only to the other. Ultimately, it is up to each reader to decide whether the ending creates a metaphor or not. If it does, most of the significance of the novel gravitates uncomfortably towards the final narrative lacuna and into the space between the last two murders. Any attempt to define the full significance of this metaphorical gap is bound to run the risk of vertigo. I shall, nevertheless, take the risk and end this chapter by exploring five possible ways of bridging the gap, the first three of which have already been tried out by some critics.

---

[17]'The apparent centre of gravity [...] is the matricide. Its true centre of gravity is the confused revolutionary who in 1936 murders Don Jesús [...] *and* the schizophrenic mind which, shortly after this "social crime", is revealed on the surface and in the subconscious depths of Pascual's confession' (73, p.19).

(1) Firstly we may adopt Sanz Villanueva's view that the historical connection is too vague to be meaningful *(63*, p.264). If Pascual's release from Chinchilla coincides with the start of the civil war, the murder of Don Jesús would be one of the many atrocities committed by psychopathic prisoners let loose on society amid the general revolutionary turmoil *(3*, p.585; *12*, pp.275–76, 278). The link between it and the matricide would be one of simple precedent, and Pascual's ending would be either involuntary or an admission of his own pathology.

(2) We could follow Sobejano *(66)* and see behind the final analogy a more positive and progressive direction, running from the matricide to Don Jesús, the abnormality of the former being subordinated to the politically more defensible killing. Unable to justify it overtly as a revolutionary act, Pascual would be using the confession as a covert form of self-justification, transferring onto the mother his hatred for Don Jesús. The omission of the last crime would offer literary resistance against the pressure to make a full confession of remorse.

(3) Following on from Osuna *(53)*, we could see the ending as a negative analogy whose direction runs backwards from the final murder to the matricide, the revolutionary killing being equated with a criminal and pathological act. If Pascual is in control of the ending, the lacuna would be an act of self-censorship and remorse, an acceptance of the Nationalists' hard-line.

(4) In a politically more neutral way we can see the final metaphor as more complex and ambiguous, with its meaning running in both directions at once, oscillating between interpretations (2) and *(3)*. The socio-political context of Don Jesús's murder would be transferred to the matricide, at the same time as the pathological hatred of the latter would be transferred to the former. Pascual would then appear as a contrite and confused revolutionary, whose previous class hatred would be challenged by his feelings of genuine remorse. The omission of the last crime would be a solution for his inner conflict of hatred and guilt.

(5) We can risk total vertigo by contemplating the possibility that the metaphorical energy generated by the ending runs not only

between the mother and Don Jesús, but also, as I have suggested, between Pascual, Cela and the reader. Pascual would not be just the representative of one side in the civil war; his behaviour would be a mirror reflecting the behaviour of all who felt justified in resorting to violence on either side. The two final victims of violence would thus acquire an additional dimension as two sides of the same coin: the mother would symbolize the reification of the enemy into a dehumanized object of hate, and the canker of a backward mother-land requiring the iron surgery of violence; Don Jesús would symbolize the same object of hatred transformed by hindsight into an idealized figure whose murder would be seen as an act of inhumanity requiring atonement.

The first three possibilities have the virtue of simplicity but are too one-sided. The fourth and fifth reflect more accurately the ambiguity of the novel's ending and the increasing symbolism acquired by the characters. The consequences for our interpretation of the author's intentions will be discussed in the Conclusion.

6. Conclusion

We have already noted the transcriber's point about our ignorance of the reasons why Pascual Duarte murdered Don Jesús González de la Riva. Given this gap in our knowledge, the whole of Pascual's story up to and including the matricide must be regarded as an explanation, or preparation, for the last omitted crime. What other reason would Pascual have for telling us about his life prior to 1922, when he is assumed to be addressing a situation arising from events in 1936? Unlike the conventional detective story where the mystery of the crime is solved at the end, in this novel, despite its apparent linearity, we are forced back to the beginning to do our own detective work in order to reconstruct the motives and mentality of the killer. Once we have uncovered a pattern of behaviour, as I tried to do in Chapter 3, the important issue then is to decide to what extent Pascual's violent actions are wilfully criminal, justified by nurture or determined by nature. At the same time we have to decide how much the significance of his violence goes beyond the purely personal and becomes political or universal. Cela himself indicates this wider dimension, and the inseparability of nature and nurture, when he describes the prehistoric roots to Pascual's behaviour in this primitive area of Spain: '¡Pobre Pascual [...] había vivido en la llana y badajoceña Torremejía, rodeado su mirar de olivos centenarios, acunada su alma por malos quereres milenarios y tostados sus cueros por un sol inclemente y viejo como el mismo mundo!' (2, p.550). Part of this echoes the idea of a racially and geographically determined national character, one which is also singled out as the novel's most important feature on the back of the Destinolibro edition with a reference to 'la barbarie ancestral de una tierra marcada por la violencia y el odio'. But Cela links the Spanish ancestry with a violence deep-rooted in human nature and nurtured by primitive conditions at any time anywhere ('un sol inclemente y viejo como el mismo mundo'); so Pascual is a Spanish version of an age-old and universal problem. Indeed what impresses about his story as a case history of violence is its modernity and continuing relevance. Besides the specific issues of criminology, penology and *machismo*, we can see that Pascual, like everybody else, needs to create something out of his life, and when frustrated he reacts badly to failure and to criticism, and without proper support from those who should be his nearest and dearest, with a tolerance of stress that is lower than most normal people's, he seems unable to cope other than in an immature and violently irrational way. Many of us may recognize these tendencies in ourselves, even though we may have learned to deal with them better than Pascual does, or rather, did in the past. Because in the present his guilt and literary self-awareness develop to produce something, a work of art, which normal readers can admire as an eminently civilized way of coping with frustration, aggression and other people's verbal venom.

This development as narrator of his own story is the most important and decisive factor in the transformation of Pascual's character; and it is one that not only connects him to equally exceptional cases in real life and to the fictional tradition of the articulate *pícaro*,[18] but also brings him increasingly closer to the reader and to Cela. As Buckley says (*19*, p.94), the picaresque form joins together protagonist, narrator and author in a mysterious trinity. But part of it is also the reader, who, besides deciding how much to identify with the first-person narrator's experience, must also consider whether the intentions of the fictional character reflect those of the hidden author. To clarify the relationship between Cela the young *señorito* and his peasant antihero, it might help to apply briefly the five hypotheses outlined in the previous chapter to interpret the end of Pascual's story. Cela's intentions would correspond to them in the following ascending order of complexity: (1)

---

[18]For example the humane treatment that produced Jimmy Boyle, *A Sense of Freedom* (London: Pan, 1977). A notable continuation of the fictional picaresque is John Banville, *The Book of Evidence* (London: Secker & Warburg, 1989). Both make good comparative reading.

the ending would be involuntary and devoid of artistic and political significance; (2) left-wing protest; (3) right-wing propaganda; (4) a liberal internalization of the conflict between left and right; and (5) the artistic complexity and political ambiguity would be shared with the narrator. The last one I prefer because its greater explanatory power can encompass the other four, but it also puts an increasing strain on the realism of Pascual's character, the plausibility of which has already been criticized by some (*35*, pp.38–39; *68*, p.295; *55*, p.376). Yet this is a necessary and deliberate consequence of the picaresque convention Cela is using, according to which the reader accepts the ability of an illiterate *pícaro* to give his worm's-eye view of reality with a degree of literary sophistication that rivals the author's (*71*, p.114). For despite Pascual's rustic self-expression (*71*, pp.105–07; *20*, p.42), his poor spelling, and the illegibility of the manuscript, his acquired mastery over language and narrative could only be explained realistically as the result, say, of education during his long period in Chinchilla prison, but in the absence of such an explanation, the effect is one of improbability, a deliberate artifice, to make a point. Pascual's split personality (half savage, half sentimental) though abnormal, is plausible in many criminals. Much more implausible is Pascual's double existence as writer and psychopath. This is where the most significant irony is generated, more significant than the different ironies rightly emphasized by Beck (*15*) and Sobejano (*66*), because it is the ambiguous irony of the picaresque (*29*, p.45; *20*, p.59), and it is brought out above all by our awareness of the story's historical context.

The guard's view that Pascual was no ordinary prisoner, (because of his extraordinary show of contrition and manic urge to write) strengthens our impression that most psychopathic revolutionaries did not, and do not, turn overnight into saints and artists. The ironic implausibility of Pascual's late death-cell transformation might of course imply that others should have followed his example; and if this were the only historical irony, then the message would be the patronisingly redemptional one of Nationalist propaganda (*53*).[19] Yet the irony is double-edged; for equally implausible

---

[19]See also Equipo Reseña, *La cultura española durante el franquismo*, ed.

potentially is the character of Pascual's last victim. The transformation of Don Jesús from object of revolutionary hatred into the
idealized object of veneration given pride of place in the dedication
may be due entirely to Pascual's change of heart. But this would
ignore the mystifying ambiguity of the dedication, and although
some may stress the futility of trying to clarify it (70, p.177; 41,
p.104), we should not leave it at that, because as Champeau says
(22, p.46) one of the pleasures of studying the text comes from our
attempt to decipher the enigma. And here I think lies the key to the
whole novel. As I argued in Chapter 4, what we see in the dedication is a superhuman gesture of forgiveness made by the victim to
his killer, one which is so disconcerting that it haunts Pascual's
memory and provokes the psychological conflict that dominates his
narrative. Moreover, the Count's gesture of forgiving his enemy can
readily be compared to Christ's attitude on the cross (16, p.317; 34,
pp.5–6; 22, p.44), and as such is in stark contrast to Pascual's
violent past and to his imminent execution in the present. But the
full irony of the dedication arises from a question imposed by the
convention of realism: does the reaction of Don Jesús have any basis
in the history of the civil war? Presumably very little. But how far is
Pascual or Cela conscious of the irony that such forgiveness was an
exception that could only prove the rule of ruthless repression?[20]
Osuna points out the improbability in Badajoz in 1936 of someone
like Pascual being allowed even to appeal against his sentence, still

Norberto Alcover (Bilbao: Mensajero, 1977), p.21.

[20]See Thomas for a possible source (12, p.271) and the reality of
repression (12, pp.259–68, 514–16, 923–25). Urrutia (71, p.66) thinks
Pascual's execution by garotte means that his killing of Don Jesús is not
political, but this implies only that the authorities regarded a revolutionary
act as that of a common criminal (see 53, p.87; 3, p.586). According to
Daniel Sueiro, *Los verdugos españoles: historia y actualidad del garrote
vil* (Madrid: Alfaguara, 1971), pp.258, 303, although the garotte had been a
common sentence in military tribunals, the Nationalists did not restore it
until 5 July 1938. Might this suggest Pascual is executed a full year after he
writes his letter? The only man Arthur Koestler remembers being garotted
while imprisoned in Seville in 1937 was, after nearly five months, the
notorious García Atadell (12, p.275). One hopes Cela will soon clarify his
sources (54, p.6).

less be left alone unmolested to write his memoirs for at least five months. For Osuna Pascual's narrative serves to whitewash the bloodiness of repression (*53*, pp.86–87), and the dedication simply shows the martyred Count's moral superiority over his enemy (*53*, pp.91–92; *64*, p.269). But if we are sensitive to ironies in the text and its context, we should at least suspect that Pascual and Cela regard the Count's gesture as totally unrepresentative (*46*, pp.136–37), exemplifying a Christian ideal of forgiveness which the régime preached but did not practise, and which, as a fictional symbol, breaks the cycle of violence taking place in reality (*22*, pp.44–45).

The Christian symbolism attached to the figure of Don Jesús connects with a corresponding symbolism in Pascual as a sacrificial lamb (*cordero pascual*) (*16*, p.313; *44*, p.39; *48*, p.8) and in his mother whose blood, he thought, tasted like a lamb's (*17*, p.81). The common symbolism suggests that all three characters are sacrificial victims of the same tragic conflict. It is at this symbolic level that the intentions of the fictional and real authors appear most to converge: in the creation of an ironic interplay between political caricature and religious idealization. The killing of Don Jesús by a grotesquely caricatured revolutionary acquires the significance of a political parricide (*53*, p.91) and a deicide (*34*, pp.4–5), the memory of which provokes the need for atonement and redemption. But the irony conveys the wish that counter-revolutionary repression might have been imposed by a more forgiving father-figure than it was at the time. As a mythified distortion of history, the novel thus provides an imaginative parody of prevailing clichés: the psychotic or contrite revolutionary (illustrated and undermined by Pascual), the evil enemy and object of hatred that has to be destroyed (symbolized by the mother and questioned by Pascual's growing guilt), and the Catholic oligarchy, crucified by revolution but responding with Christian concern for the souls of the defeated (represented by Don Jesús and belied by Pascual's execution).

So a final tentative definition of Cela's and Pascual's intentions would be this: at a time of acute polarization when moral and political issues were appallingly clear-cut, the two authors on opposite sides of the conflict (the *señorito* and the *campesino*) find not just a common cause in their guilt (*19*, pp.98–99) but also a common purpose in blurring the issues and uniting the extremes through the deliberate creation of narrative irony and moral ambiguity (*33*, p.122), the ultimate intention of their story being to provoke readers to examine their consciences and try to understand their own and the enemy's aggression.[21] The effect is one of tragic catharsis through ironic reversal: the emotional and moral polarization, with all the horror focused on the evil mother and all the pity focused on the Christ-like Don Jesús, is reversed by a metaphorical identification of the two enemies (with a corresponding identification behind them of protagonist and author/reader). For those prepared to feel identified, Pascual's story reflected the psychopathology of a society still suffering the traumatic aftermath of civil war, and provided a form of collective therapy, a means of escaping the fatality of violence through the act of communication (*22*, pp.38, 40). By imposing on himself and his readers a picaresque complicity (*74*, p.23) and an ironic confraternity (*29*, pp.38, 44) with a murderous victim of the Nationalist Crusade, Cela tried at least in fiction to fulfil, however ambiguously, the Christian injunction to 'Love your enemies', whilst forcing the reader to share Pascual's conviction that the enemy's evil fully justifies hatred.

The novel made its tremendous impact because it caused a therapeutic shock to the system, in a literary, psychological and cultural sense. The so-called *tremendismo* (with its brutal mixture of sex and violence) is certainly sensationalist, but its presence here is also artistically subtle, because to the violent content are added structural violations which make the novel doubly disconcerting. Cela thus introduced an important dimension of formal experimentation which is not emphasized enough in even the most perceptive definitions of *tremendismo* (e.g.*10*, pp.323–24; *39*, pp.16, 21). This helps resolve the contradiction between those who claim the novel's violence reflected the ideology of Francoism (*9*, pp.42–43) and those

---

[21]For psychological polarization as a cause of violence see Anthony Storr, *Human Destructiveness* (London: Chatto & Windus, 1972), p.87; and *34*, pp.2–3.

who argue that its violent discourse was in some equally vague way
a literary protest against the regime (*71*, pp.102, 107–08; *31*, pp.4,
7); for the novel's formal presentation through documents is
subversive of all authoritarian discourses, encouraging readers to
think for themselves and read between the lines (*15*, p.284; *22*,
pp.18–22), but especially between the gaps, those between past and
present and text and context. In suppressing the one crime
connected to the civil war, the novel subjects that violence to an
extraordinary process of literary transformation, by virtue of which
the violence becomes enigmatic, displaced, internalized, and finally
sublimated into the creative tension of art.

I should like to finish this Critical Guide by returning to the
passage already quoted in the Introduction, the one in which Cela
recounts how ill-health forced him to bring the novel to a premature
end so the manuscript would not be left as a useless family souvenir,
'no más que como un triste e inútil recuerdo familiar' (*2*, p.551). By
'recuerdo familiar' Cela obviously refers to his own family; but
there is enough ambiguity about the phrase to suggest a reference
also to Pascual's family. And the main reason why the novel
achieved fame for the author is because Pascual's memory of his
family life acquires an extra dimension of historical significance
precisely through the means Cela used to bring it to its premature
end: the lacuna in which story and history finally collide. Forced to
curtail the full prosaic development of events normally expected in
the conventional well-told tale, Cela had to use the poetic short-cut
of metaphor to connect a grotesqe family story with the historical
tragedy. The result was not a lengthy sustained novel, but, in my
view, one that is powerfully short, mimetically distorting, psychologically explosive, and, last but not least, artistically enduring.
Although one critic has referred to the 'poetic technique' that
'leaves much to the reader's imagination' (*26*, p.658), many may
still feel that too much is left to the imagination, a worry that was
voiced in fact even before the novel's publication when Cela sent
the manuscript to the *Revista de Occidente* and received a letter

(dated 11 February 1942) in which Fernando Vela wrote: 'Novela es la descripción de un círculo completo de vida, sin huecos ni vacíos, como es el que realmente rodea a cada uno de nosotros, el mundo propio de cada cual' (2, p.552). Cela's own comment ('Puede que tenga razón') shows himself prepared to countenance criticism of the gaps in his novel. Nevertheless, while he continued looking for a publisher during the rest of 1942, he left the work as it was, satisfied no doubt with the literary effectiveness of the premature ending, and its capacity to do what Cela has always liked doing, to disconcert his readers.

The resulting lack of an explicit and sustained connection between story and history is certainly a major defect for some critics (*13; 63*). I have tried to argue that the final gap is a virtue from both an esthetic and ethical point of view, even though I am aware that the novel's conjunction of a private family squabble and the national tragedy threatens to view the latter from what apppears to be a grossly narrow angle. This is perhaps most apparent in the way Pascual's story centres on his violence as a personal, psychological, problem, to the exclusion of precisely those aspects of his life that might be more relevant to the socio-historical conflict, such as his work and his relationships with people outside his closed family circle. For we are told next to nothing about his place in the wider economical and political structure of his village and region. This matters less if we attempt to see an analogy between his failure to produce a family and similar frustrations in the socio-economic sphere, though there is little explicit support for this in the text. Such blatant depoliticization of Pascual's life, followed by its last-minute insertion in a confused and distorted historical context, is too hard to swallow for those who like Osuna consider the ending politically arbitrary, not artistically complex (*53*, p.94). If the novel had concentrated more on these other aspects it might have been easier to digest for many (though certainly not for the censors). But the main virtue of focusing on Pascual's abnormal psychology is exactly that: psychological. For we are compelled to feel involved in the same emotional and mental processes as Pascual through the narrative form Cela had the brilliant idea of using: the first-person picaresque. This ensures that the family referred to in the novel's title is not limited to Pascual's home in Torremejía, nor even to the wider social family in a class sense; it includes within its disturbing embrace a whole family of people united and divided by a common psychology of violent hatred. It thus exposed to view, in 1942, the strife-torn reality behind the Francoist facade of the ideal Christian family.[22] Pascual clearly comes from a family of *marginados*, socially and geographically remote from the centres of power and privilege (*10*; *62*, p.9). But his 'pueblo perdido' (p.21) was in 1936 at the centre of historical action. Appropriately, the novelist's imagination brings the black, forgotten, sheep of the family back from the margins to the centre of national consciousness, and allows him to rejoin the human race, the family of man, from which he has excluded himself through matricide. His autobiography thus held up a mirror for readers to recognize not just a flawed society but also their own flawed humanity (*74*, pp.49–50).

This for me is the work's central achievement: to have transformed a violent historical conflict into an internal psychological conflict, a literary experience rich in ambivalence and ambiguity, proving that literature has something valuable to say about human aggression. Doubts will remain as to whether Pascual is cured by art or remains incurable. But whether we see him as a sacrificial lamb or a wolf in sheep's clothing is ultimately an important matter of literary uncertainty. What is certain is that Cela created in him a very uncomfortable bed-fellow for both himself and his readers. The content of his character and Cela's formal presentation of it have provoked outrage, bewilderment, admiration, and intense critical interest. May they long continue to do so; for instead of a clear message the novel leaves us with exemplary questions. Should

---

[22]The law of 18 July 1938 begins: 'Es consigna rigurosa de nuestra Revolución elevar y fortalecer la familia en su tradición cristiana, sociedad natural y perfecta y cimiento de la Nación' (María Carmen García-Nieto and Javier Mª Donézar, *Bases documentales de la España contemporánea, X: La guerra de España, 1936–1939* (Madrid: Guadiana, 1974), p.381.

someone get away with murder? Is there good in even the worst of us? Are things always what they seem to be? Is it better not to jump to conclusions? That is why this one remains tentative.[23]

---

[23]These conclusions are not altered by the latest instalment of Cela's autobiography, *Memorias, entendimientos y voluntades* (Barcelona: Plaza & Janés, 1993). This clarifies many of his movements and attitudes before, during and after the civil war. But, apart from a fragmentary description of his army posting to Pascual's village in February and March 1939 (in the chapter 'Torremejía') and the emphasis given to the illness that precipitated the novel's end (in the chapter 'Mi primera novela'), the precise links between reality and fiction remain tantalizingly unclear.

Bibliographical Note

Abbreviations:
FPD   *La familia de Pascual Duarte*
PD   Pascual Duarte
CJC   Camilo José Cela
H   *Hispania* (U.S.A.)
REH   *Revista de Estudios Hispánicos* (U.S.A.)

A EDITIONS

1. Boudreau, Harold L., and John W. Kronik (New York: Appleton-Century-Crofts, 1961). Has a useful introd.
2. Cela, Camilo José, in his *La obra completa de CJC*, I (Barcelona: Destino, 1962). The 13th, definitive, edition established by Cela with variants, a new preface 'Pascual Duarte de limpio', and two important old ones, 'Andanzas europeas y americanas de Pascual Duarte y su familia' and (from *1*) 'Palabras ocasionales'.
3. Entrambasaguas, Joaquín de, in *Las mejores novelas contemporáneas*, X (Barcelona: Planeta, 1966). The introd. stresses PD's brutality and Cela's skill, pp.580–90.
4. Urrutia, Jorge (Barcelona: Planeta, 1977). An excellent edition unlikely to be reprinted; its introd. is available as (*71*).

B TRANSLATIONS

5. *Pascual Duarte's Family* (London: Eyre & Spottiswoode, 1947). Translation and prologue by John Marks.
6. *The Family of Pascual Duarte* (New York: Avon/Bard, 1966). Translation and afterword by Anthony Kerrigan.
7. *The Family of Pascual Duarte* (1964; rpt. Boston: Little, Brown, [1990]). Kerrigan's translation, his afterword now the introd.

C BACKGROUND

8. Brown, G. G. *A Literary History of Spain: The Twentieth Century* (London: Ernest Benn, 1972). See p.145.

9. Marfany, Joan-Lluís. 'Notes sobre la novel.la espanyola de postguerra', *Els Marges*, no.6 (1976), 29–57. On the ideology of *tremendismo*, accuses Cela of an esthetic game of violent irrationalism, dismissing his nonconformity as a Falangist intellectual's sour grapes.

10. Morán, Fernando. *Novela y semidesarrollo* (Madrid: Taurus, 1971). Links PD's primitive insecurity to socio-historical marginalization and discontinuity, pp. 317–23.

11. Rodríguez Puértolas, Julio. *Literatura fascista española*, I: *Historia* (Madrid: Akal, 1986). On CJC, pp.584–609; on *FPD*, pp.590–94. Favours Osuna's line (*53*).

12. Thomas, Hugh. *The Spanish Civil War*, 3rd ed. (Harmondsworth: Penguin, 1977).

D CRITICISM

13. Alborg, Juan Luis. *Hora actual de la novela española* (Madrid: Taurus, 1958). On Cela, pp.79–87 and 110–13; argues that the novel's impressive style and sensational impact have concealed its lack of substance, unconvincing plot and implausible characterization.

14. Bache Cortés, Yolanda. *'FPD*: ¿Historia de un matricidio?', in Bache Cortés, and Irma I. Fernández Arias, *Pascual Duarte y Alfanhuí: dos actitudes de posguerra* (México: UNAM, 1979), pp.1–51. Rhapsodic defence of PD as victim and killer.

15. Beck, Mary Ann. 'Nuevo encuentro con *FPD*', *Revista Hispánica Moderna*, 30 (1964), 279–98. Acutely stresses the ironic discrepancy between PD's words and deeds; a necessary antidote to explanations absolving him of all moral responsibility.

16. Bernstein, J. S. 'PD and Orestes', *Symposium*, 22 (1968), 301–18. A good attempt to trace a mythic parallel, seeing the last crime as one against the State; too much on matriarchy, no mention of tragedy.

17. 'The Matricide of Pascual Duarte', in *Homenaje a Rodríguez-Moñino* (Madrid: Castalia, 1966), I, pp.75–82. Discusses the females as sexual taboo figures.

18. Breiner-Sanders, Karen E. *'FPD' a través de su imaginería* (Madrid: Pliegos, 1990). Systematic study of the imagery, underlining the good and bad in PD; dismisses Beck's view of irony (*15*) and reduces the textual ambiguity to a simple view of PD as social victim.

19. Buckley, Ramón. *Raíces tradicionales de la novela contemporánea en España* (Barcelona: Península, 1982). Ch.2 (i), 'El pícaro como criminal: *FPD (Cela, 1942)*', pp.92–99. Convincingly sees the picaresque protagonist's self-transformation through narrative as a projection of Cela's own guilt from the same civil war context.

20. ——, *Edición de 'FPD': CJC* (Madrid: Alborada, 1989). Not an edition, but a useful exercise-book guide for secondary schools.

21. Busette, Cedric. 'FPD and the Prominence of Fate', *REH*, 8 (1974), 61–67. Lists the many instances of fate.

22. Champeau, Geneviève. 'Nueva lectura de *FPD*', *Iris* (Montpellier), no.1 (1985), 15–52. Excellent study of the civil war and social context, stressing PD's narrative therapy and remorse; but ignores the ambiguity and irony.

23. Castellet, J.M. 'Iniciación a la obra narrativa de CJC', *Revista Hispánica Moderna*, 28 (1962), 107–50. Says PD's brutality is conditioned by society, pp.125–29.

24. Dougherty, Dru. 'Pascual en la cárcel: el encubierto relato de *FPD*', *Insula*, no.365 (April 1977), 5, 7. Excellent on the importance of PD's self-liberation as narrator and the complex structure.

25. Dyer, Mary Julia. '*L'étranger* y *FPD*: un contraste de conceptos', *Papeles de Son Armadans*, 44, no.132 (March 1967), 265–301. Lucidly defines the differences, emphasizing PD's goodness, fate, and the *tremendista* antecedent of *Cintas Rojas*.

26. Feldman, David M. 'CJC and *FPD*', *H*, 44 (1961), 656–59. Perceptive on PD's existential responsibility and *Chispa*, but less so on the importance of Don Jesús.

27. Foster, David W. *Forms of the Novel in the Work of CJC* (Columbia: Univ. of Missouri Press, 1967). Ch. 1, 'FPD: The Novel in a Traditional Form', pp.16–33. Usefully discusses problems of autobiographical form; says PD's guilt is ironical because society is to blame.

28. George, David. 'The Theme of the Journey in Cela's *FPD*', *Quinquereme* (Bath), 3 (1980), 101–10. Three journeys show the impossibility of flight from disaster.

29. Giménez-Frontín, José Luis. *CJC: texto y contexto* (Barcelona: Montesinos, 1985). Ch. 2, 'De falsos pícaros y confesiones falsas', pp.29-47. Stresses the crucial omission of Don Jesús, and rejects the idea (*19*) of PD as a projection of Cela's guilt.

30. González, Bernardo A. *Parábolas de identidad* (Potomac: Scripta Humanistica, 1985). Studies the swing between aggression and confession, inconclusively, pp.22–46.

31. Gullón, Germán. 'Contexto ideológico y forma narrativa en *FPD*: en busca de una perspectiva lectorial', *H*, 68 (1985), 1–8. Curiously says critical condemnation of PD has been insufficient whilst the transcriber's is too Francoist; perceptive on PD's narrative escape from linguistic repression.

32. ——, 'La figura del narratario: un ejemplo español (Cela)', in *Crítica semiológica de textos literarios hispánicos*, ed. M. A. Garrido Gallardo (Madrid: Consejo Superior de Investigaciones Científicas,

1986), pp.591–601. A shortened version of (*31*).

33. Hoyle, Alan. 'PD y el cementerio de Torremejía', *Nueva Estafeta* (Madrid), no.27 (February 1981), 118–22. Studies the complexities of PD's past and present in Chs 5 and 17, and the historical reality of the setting.

34. ——, '*FPD*: psicoanálisis de la historia', in *Actas del VIII Congreso de la Asociación Internacional de Hispanistas (Brown University, 22–27 agosto 1983)*, ed. A. David Kossoff and others (Madrid: Istmo, 1986), II, pp.1–11. Exploring the narrative as a Freudian therapy for PD's double Oedipus complex, tries to bridge the gap between psychology and history.

35. Ilie, Paul. *La novelística de CJC* (Madrid: Gredos, 1963). Ch.1, '*FPD*', pp.36–76. A pioneering study of PD's primitive inarticulateness; sees the violence as existential and esthetic.

36. 'La lectura del "vagabundaje" de Cela en la época posfranquista', *Cuadernos Hispanoamericanos*, 113 (July–August 1978), pp.61–80. Recognizes a vague socio-historical dimension, at pp.52–53, 62–63, 66, 148.

37. *Insula*, nos 518–19 (February–March 1990). Includes: (*50*); P. Abad Contreras, 'Bibliografía de CJC. Cuaderno de trabajo', pp.i–viii; and Jorge Urrutia, 'El manuscrito de FPD', pp.68–69.

38. Jerez-Farrán, Carlos. 'PD y la susceptibilidad viril', *Hispanófila*, no.95 (January 1989), 47–63. Convincingly explains PD's violence as male insecurity, connecting *machismo* socio-anthropologically to domestic matriarchy and political patriarchy; flawed by reductive dismissal of PD's narrative as merely cynical.

39. Jones, Margaret E. W. *The Contemporary Spanish Novel, 1939–1975*, Twayne World Authors Series, 752 (Boston: Twayne, 1985). Covers *tremendismo*, pp.15–18, and *FPD*, pp.18–21.

40. Kronik, John W. 'Pascual's Parole', *Review of Contemporary Fiction* (Elmwood Park, IL), 4, no.3 (1984), 111–19. With a nice pun on *parole*, studies PD's existential imprisonment and narrative self-creation.

41. Livingstone, Leon. 'Ambivalence and Ambiguity in *FPD*', in *Studies in Honor of José Rubia Barcia*, ed. Roberta Johnson and Paul C. Smith (Lincoln, NE: Society of Spanish and Spanish-American Studies, 1982), pp.95–107. Excellent on PD's two-sided character and, less clearly, his 'ambivalent ambiguity' towards language and fate.

42. Lottini, Otello. 'La scrittura e l'enigma: su *FPD* di CJC', *Linguistica e Letteratura*, 5 (1980), 29–60. Limited structuralist focus on the contextual documents and linguistic act; claims PD usurps Cela's role and the death of Don Jesús symbolizes that of the author.

43. ——, 'Il silenzio e la parola: su *FPD* di CJC', *Linguistica e Letteratura*, 12 (1987), 185–216. Deals with PD's lack of communication, with no advance on (*35*).

44. McPheeters, D. W. *CJC*, Twayne World Authors Series, 67 (New York: Twayne, 1969). Ch.2, pp.31–51. Sensible discussion of the plot, Don Jesús, Marañón's defence, *tremendismo* and *L'Etranger*.

45. Marañón, Gregorio. 'Prólogo' to *FPD*, 4th ed. (Barcelona: Zodíaco, 1946), pp.1–17. (Reproduced in *Insula*, no.5 (May 1946), 1, 3, and the Destino editions (Barcelona, 1951–60)). Cleverly presented as two men debating the morality of PD's primitive justice and insinuating the contemporary relevance of the tragedy.

46. Marban, Jorge A. *Camus y Cela: el drama del antihéroe trágico* (Barcelona: Picazo, 1973). Illustrates differences more than similarities; argues that society is guilty for neglecting PD.

47. Marín Martínez, Juan María. 'Sentido último de *FPD*', *Cuadernos Hispanoamericanos*, 113 (1978), 90–98. A simplistic discussion of tragedy ignoring PD's guilt; sees Don Jesús's murder as a rebellion against social destiny.

48. Masoliver Ródenas, Juan Antonio. 'PD y el capítulo trece', *Los Cuadernos del Norte* (Oviedo), no.15 (September-October 1982), 4–9. Stressing Ch.13 and narrative therapy, sees a parody of the Holy Family, PD identifying himself with Christ, and the violence as Oedipal.

49. ——, 'La inmolación de PD', *Las Nuevas Letras* (Almería), no.6 (Winter 1987), 57–64. Sees an Oedipal obsession with maternity, and the same crucifixion symbolism as (*48*).

50. ——, 'Las dos lecturas de *FPD*' (*37*, pp.51–52). Largely a reworking of (*49*).

51. Montes-Huidobro, Matías. 'Dinámica de la correlación existencial en *FPD*', *REH*, 16 (1982), 213–22. Sees existentialism in PD's love of objects, alienation from people, and violence on returning from somewhere.

52. Nora, Eugenio G. de. *La novela española contemporánea (1927–1960)* (Madrid: Gredos, 1962), II.ii, pp.113–17. Notes PD's bizarre character, more sinned against by society than sinning.

53. Osuna, Rafael. 'PD: asesino, miliciano, nacionalista', *Ideologies & Literature*, no.11 (1979), 82–96. Perceptive and challenging discussion of the historical context to the last murder, whose omission is seen as a distortion to serve Nationalist propaganda.

54. *Papeles de Son Armadans*, 48, no.142 (January 1968). Special number on *FPD*; includes (*66*) and Cela's preface, 'Inevitable, rigurosamente inevitable', pp.5–8.

55. Penuel, Arnold M. 'The Psychology of Cultural Disintegration in

Cela's *FPD'*, *REH*, 16 (1982), 361–78. Makes use of depth
psychology and Ortega to link PD's violence with pre-war society.

56. Pérez Minik, Domingo. *Novelistas españoles de los siglos XIX y XX*
(Madrid: Guadarrama, 1957). '*FPD*, CJC', pp. 258–69, is acute on the
historical background and the difference between *FPD* and
L'Etranger.

57. Picard, Hans Rudolf. 'Narrative Präsentation zwischen Fiktion und
Wirklichkeit in CJCs FPD: die sinnkonstituierende Leistung der
Beziehung zwischen Rahmen und Text', in *Aspekte der Hispania im
19. und 20. Jahrhundert: Akten des deutschen Hispanistentages 1983*,
ed. Dieter Kremer (Hamburg: Buske, 1983), pp. 69–77. Sees Don
Jesús as a symbol of sacrificial love redeeming hatred, underlined by
smile and look motifs.

58. *La picaresca: orígenes, textos y estructuras: Actas del I Congreso
Internacional sobre la Picaresca*, ed. M. Criado de Val (Madrid:
Fundación Universitaria Española, 1979). Includes: Anthony N.
Zahareas, 'El género picaresco y las autobiografías de criminales',
pp.79–111 (informative); Ignacio Soldevila-Durante, 'Utilización de la
tradición picaresca por CJC', pp.921–28 (compares the more creative
FPD with the lifeless *Nuevas andanzas y desventuras de Lazarillo de
Tormes*); Hortensia Viñes, 'Notas para una interpretación de *PD*: La
novela virtual', pp.929–34 (says virtually nothing).

59. Rodríguez, Alfred, and John Timms. 'El significado de lo femenino en
FPD', *REH*, 11 (1977), 251–64. Flimsily claims the novel destroys a
feminine ideal.

60. Rosenberg, John R. 'El autobiógrafo encerrado: PD y su transcriptor',
Explicación de Textos Literarios, 14, no.2 (1985–86), 63–72.
Reconciles PD's narrative therapy with the transcriber's manipulation
and preservation of the MS.

61. ——, 'PD and the Eye of the Beholder: Cela, Sartre, and the
Metaphor of Vision', *Revista Canadiense de Estudios Hispánicos*, 14
(1989–90), 149–60. Unconvincing Sartrean study of PD's visual inter-
actions.

62. Sagaró Faci, Matilde. *Claves de 'FPD': CJC* (Madrid: Ciclo, 1990).
Potted summary and superficial commentary.

63. Sanz Villanueva, Santos. *Historia de la novela social española
(1942–1975)*, I (Madrid: Alhambra, 1980). Excellent survey of criticism and background, emphasizing the individual over the political,
and rural drama over the picaresque, pp. 247–66.

64. Schaefer, Claudia. 'Conspiración, manipulación, conversión ambigua:
PD y la utopía histórica del Nuevo Estado español', *Anales de la
Literatura Española Contemporánea*, 13 (1988), 261–81. Informative
consolidation of (*53*), but mistakenly assumes that PD's confession to

the chaplain precedes his text.

65. Sherzer, William M. 'Primitivism in *FPD*', *Discurso Literario* (Stillwater), 5 (1987–88), 473–82. Using Malinowski and Freud, claims there is a central conflict between sister love and mother hatred.

66. Sobejano, Gonzalo. 'Reflexiones sobre *FPD*', in (*54*, pp.19–58). Excellent, seminal, socio-historical interpretation, stressing Don Jesús, and the novel's place in post-war realism. (A shortened, modified, version appears in his *Novela española de nuestro tiempo (en busca del pueblo perdido)*, 2nd ed. (Madrid: Prensa Española, 1975), pp.91–106).

67. Soldevila Durante, Ignacio. *La novela desde 1936* (Madrid: Alhambra, 1980). Emphasizes irony and contradictions, pp.109–11.

68. Spires, Robert C. 'Systematic Doubt: The Moral Art of *FPD*', *Hispanic Review*, 40 (1972), 283–302. Influential analysis of narrative ambiguities, limited by its emphasis on the transcriber and exclusion of Don Jesús.

69. —— 'La dinámica tonal de *FPD*', in his *La novela española de posguerra* (Madrid: Cupsa, 1978), pp. 24–51. Drawing on (*68*) and his article (*Insula*, no.298, September 1971) argues that three key incidents show PD's existential self-affirmation.

70. Thomas, Michael D. 'Narrative Tension and Structural Unity in Cela's *FPD*', *Symposium*, 31 (1977), 165–78. Usefully studies PD's emotional conflict as narrator, but focuses exclusively on the mother.

71. Urrutia, Jorge. *Cela: FPD (Los contextos y el texto)* (Madrid: Sociedad General Española de Librería, 1982). A well-documented, often illuminating, study of the cultural context and narrative structure; sees the discourse of violence as a protest against post-war repression.

72. Vernon, Kathleen M. '*La Politique des Auteurs*: Narrative Point of View in *PD*, Novel and Film', *H*, 72 (1989), 87–96. Sophisticated theory, but prefers the film's crude historicization to the novel's subtle irony.

73. Yates, Alan. 'The First-Person Narrative Mode in *FPD* and *Nada*', *Vida Hispánica*, no.3 (Autumn 1976), 11–20. A perceptive note of caution against PD's subjectivity.

74. Zamora Vicente, Alonso. *CJC: acercamiento a un escritor* (Madrid: Gredos, 1962). '*FPD*', pp.23–50. A fragmentary study of PD's sensitive side, lucidly hinting at historical depth beneath the violent surface.

CRITICAL GUIDES TO SPANISH TEXTS

Edited by
J.E. Varey, A.D. Deyermond and C. Davies

CRITICAL GUIDES TO SPANISH TEXTS

Edited by
J.E. Varey, A.D. Deyermond and C. Davies